A Communicative Grammar

interactions access

A Communicative Grammar

interactions access

Second Edition

Patricia K. Werner

John P. Nelson
Monterey Peninsula College

Marilynn Spaventa
Santa Barbara City College

With Contributions by
Miki Prijic Knezevic

The McGraw-Hill Companies, Inc.
New York St. Louis San Francisco Auckland Bogotá Caracas Lisbon London Madrid Mexico City Milan Montreal New Delhi San Juan Singapore Sydney Tokyo Toronto

This is an EBI book.

McGraw-Hill
A Division of The McGraw-Hill Companies

Interactions Access
A Communicative Grammar
Second Edition

This book is printed on acid-free paper.

3 4 5 6 7 8 9 0 DOC DOC 9 0 9 8

ISBN 0-07-069603-9

This book was set in Times Roman by The Clarinda Company.
The editors were Tim Stookesberry and Bill Preston;
the editing manager was Ira C. Roberts;
the production supervisor was Annette Mayeski;
the designer was Francis Owens.
The cover was designed by Francis Owens and Kathryn Meehan.
The cover illustrator was Zita Asbaghi.
The photo editor was Elyse Rieder.
Project supervision was done by The Clarinda Company.
R. R. Donnelley & Sons Company was printer and binder.

Photo credits: *Page 1* © Peter Menzel/Stock, Boston; *27* © Malyszko/Stock, Boston; *37* © Walter Gilardetti; *48* © Latin Focus; *61* © Courtesy Patty Werner; *69* © Courtesy Patty Werner; *77* © Courtesy Patty Werner; *92* © E. Williamson/Picture Cube; *92* © Jeffry Myers/Stock, Boston; *98* © Courtesy Patty Werner; *99* © Courtesy of Peggy Hill; *101* © Tim Davis/Photo Researchers; *131* © Michael Grecco/Stock, Boston; *133* © Judy Gelles/Stock, Boston; *133* © Bill Bachman/Photo Researchers; *139* © Bettmann; *139* © (no credit listed in previous ed.); *139* © AP/Wide World Photos; *144* © John P. Nelson; *145* © John P. Nelson; *145* © AP/Wide World Photos; *152* © AP/Wide World Photos; *163* © Joel Gordon; *166* © Len Rue, Jr./Monkmeyer; *168* © Bruce Roberts/Photo Researchers; *168* © National Museum of American Art: gift of Mrs. Joseph Harrison, Jr.; *172* © Corbis-Bettmann; *176* © Rafael Macia/Photo Researchers; *178* © Bernard Bison/Stock, Boston; *180* © Granitsas/Image Works; *185* © AP/Wide World Photos; *193* © Ken Karp/Omni-Photo Communications; *206* © Rafael Macia/Photo Researchers; *216* © Jim Harrison/Stock, Boston; *216* © AP/Wide World Photos; *217* © Michael Dwyer/Stock, Boston; *241* © Jim Whitmer/Stock, Boston; *268* © AP/Wide World Photos; *268* © AP/Wide World Photos; *271* © Courtesy NASA; *281* © Rogers/Monkmeyer; *281* © Weston Kemp; *288* © Kagan/Monkmeyer; *294* © AP/Wide World Photos; *296* © AP/Wide World Photos; *297* © Peter Menzel/Stock, Boston; *297* © Alice Grossman/Picture Cube; *297* © Victor Englebert/Photo Researchers; *297* © AP/Wide World Photos.

http://www.mhcollege.com

Contents

CHAPTER ten

Our Planet 271

Appendixes 303

Preface
to the Second Edition

The Interactions Access Program

The Interactions Access program consists of four texts and a variety of supplemental materials for beginning to high-beginning students seeking to improve their English language skills. Each of the four texts in this program is carefully organized by chapter theme, vocabulary, grammar structures, and, where possible, language functions. As a result, information introduced in a chapter of any one of the Interactions Access texts corresponds to and reinforces material taught in the same chapter of the other three books, creating a truly integrated, four-skills approach.

The Interactions Access program is highly flexible. The texts in this series may be used together or separately, depending on students' needs and course goals. The books in this program include:

- **A Communicative Grammar.** This book is organized by grammatical structures, all of which are presented, practiced, and applied in context. Grammar is presented in manageable sections, starting with simple material and gradually working up to more complex structures. In each chapter, students are led through a logical, complete presentation in which grammar points are consistently recycled and reinforced. Exercises following each grammar presentation proceed from controlled to open-ended. Like the other three books in this series, the grammar book includes a variety of communicative activities that are enhanced by visuals and realia. Through its conversational approach, this book helps students *use* the grammar structures they are studying in *real-life* communication.

- **A Reading/Writing Book.** The reading selections in this text are carefully graded in level. While the readings are not difficult, the topics are more sophisticated than those found in most low-level readers. Vocabulary is recycled from chapter to chapter to provide reinforcement. Reading skills such as skimming, scanning, and finding meaning from context are emphasized to help students understand the structure and organization of each reading. Writing sections include prewriting activities and specific writing tasks, followed by editing practice, peer feedback, and journal writing topics. To build students' confidence, chapters begin with highly controlled types of exercises and activities and build to freer, more communicative ones.

- **A Listening/Speaking Book.** This book uses lively, natural language from a variety of contexts. Listening materials include formal and informal conversations, interviews, lectures, announcements, and recorded messages. Speaking activities include role play, small-group activities, and classroom discussions. Listening strategies include making predictions, taking notes, drawing inferences, and listening for stressed words, reduced forms, and intonation.

- **A Multi-Skills Activity Book.** New to this edition, this text gives students integrated practice in all four language skills. Among the communicative activities included in this text are exercises for the new video program that accompanies the Interactions Access program.

Supplemental Materials

In addition to the four texts outlined above, various supplemental materials are available to assist users of the second edition, including:

Instructor's Manual

Extensively revised for the new edition, this manual provides instructions and guidelines for using the four texts separately or in various combinations to suit particular program needs. For each of the texts, there is a separate section with answer keys, teaching tips, and a comprehensive sample test.

Audio Program for *Interactions Access: A Listening/Speaking Book*

Completely rerecorded for the new edition, the audio program is designed to be used in conjunction with those exercises that are indicated with a cassette icon in the student text. Complete tapescripts are now included in the back of the student text.

Audio Program for *Interactions Access: A Reading/Writing Book*

This new optional audio cassette contains readings from the student text. These taped selections enable students to listen at their leisure to the natural oral discourse of native readers for intonation and modeling. Readings included in this program are indicated with a cassette icon in the student text.

Video

New to this edition, the video program for Interactions Access contains authentic television segments that are coordinated with the ten chapter themes in the four texts. Exercises and activities for this video are in the Multi-Skills Activity Book.

Interactions Access: A Communicative Grammar, Second Edition

Rationale

Interactions Access: A Communicative Grammar, Second Edition, introduces practices, and applies basic grammatical structures in everyday contexts. The beginning chapters are controlled for structure and vocabulary. The later chapters shift to a wider range of exercises and activities involving more vocabulary.

The text is organized by structure and theme. The first several chapters concentrate on key structures (the verb *be*, present tenses, and some modal auxiliaries) while building a core of high-frequency vocabulary through contexts such as nutrition, North American history and geography, work and leisure, and world issues.

Chapter Organization

Chapters are divided into topics representing one or two days of class work and homework. Each topic opens with artwork and a short reading selection or conversation that introduces the theme and target structures. Grammar cxplanations and exercises follow each opening selection. Activities that focus on the target structures are also included at the end of each topic section. (See **Using What You've Learned** on page xi.)

Introductory Readings/Conversations

The topic openers can be used to introduce key vocabulary and to make sure that students have a basic understanding of the topic material. The introductory selection can be covered with the class as a whole, or it can be used as a homework assignment or a listening comprehension exercise.

Grammar Explanations

Examples are given for each grammatical structure covered in the text. Explanations have been kept to a minimum to avoid using too much "teacher talk" in the text. Instructors are encouraged to supplement the explanatory material in the text *if* a particular class is ready and able to handle explanations in more detail.

Exercises

Every topic includes a variety of exercises that are sequenced to progress from more-controlled to less-controlled practice of the target structures. The exercises are both traditional and innovative, including sentence completions, transformation, chain drills, sentence combining, question-answer sequences, and information gaps (see below). Most exercises can be used as either oral or written work, and many can be done in pairs or groups as well as with the entire class.

Information Gaps

These communicative activities are meant to be done orally in pairs. Each student is given part of the information required to complete a particular task and should look only at his or her own information. Then, by listening and speaking in turn, students exchange their information to successfully complete the task (bridge the information gap).

Using What You've Learned

Interactions Access: A Communicative Grammar includes over forty speaking and writing activities, role plays, language games, and tasks. These activities appear at the end of every topic in a section called **Using What You've Learned.** These activities are optional, but we recommend using as many as possible. The activities highlight the functional roles of structures covered in each topic, and they give students regular opportunities to actively practice the material in natural, personalized, interactive ways.

Review

The text offers a great deal of review. Exercises review structures throughout the text. In addition, Chapters Two, Four, Six, Eight, and Ten have a special section called "Checking Your Progress." These progress checks have a two-part, multiple-choice format. Each covers a variety of structures from the previous two chapters. Finally, Chapters Five and Ten have a fourth topic devoted to general review.

Flexibility

Because ESOL courses vary greatly in length and focus, this text may include more material than necessary for some courses. If you do not have time to cover all the material in the text, be selective. Cover structures that the majority of your students have the most difficulty with, and omit or de-emphasize structures that most students can already use reasonably well. In addition, you may choose to omit review material, readings, and activities. Of course, this material may be assigned to those students who need additional work with given structures, or it may be used as the basis for quizzes or tests.

New to the Second Edition

1. **Streamlined Design.** The new edition features an attractive two-color design and an extensively revised art program.
2. **Checking Your Progress.** These new boxed features appear at the end of Chapters Two, Four, Six, Eight, and Ten. They are designed to help students review and check their progress with key grammar structures every two chapters. At the same time, they help students become more familiar with multiple-choice formats for standardized tests that are commonly used in North America.

3. **Culture Notes.** These new features, appearing in every chapter, describe interesting or unusual aspects of North American culture related to the chapter theme.
4. **Additional Grammar structures.** The new edition features a range of new material in Chapter Ten. Chapter Ten introduces common uses of the past participle: as adjectives, in the present perfect tense, and in passive constructions.
5. **Reference Appendixes.** In the new edition, key reference material has been consolidated in special appendixes, making it easier to find. In addition, more irregular verbs are included and past participles are also given for all irregular verbs covered in the text.

Acknowledgments

We would like to thank all the special people who helped us with this book, especially Mary Gill, Elaine Goldberg, Roseanne, Mendoza, Tim Stookesberry, and Bill Preston, without whose tireless efforts this book would not have been possible. And we would like to give resounding applause to those who put up with us during this event: Alfonso, Alex, Martin, and Camilla; Susan and Marina; Lou, Louisa, John, and Katie.

Introduction

To The Students and the Teacher

Welcome to your new English class. This book will help you practice grammatical structures and learn new vocabulary at the same time.

To begin, learn about the other students in your class. What are their names? Where are they from? Here are some expressions to help you.

Expressions

QUESTIONS	ANSWERS
What is your name?	My name is ________.
Where are you from?	I am from ________.
What nationality are you?	I am ________.
What is your native (first) language?	My native language is ________.

activity Walk around the classroom. Talk to the other students. Ask them questions. Use the expressions in the box, and the cartoon, map, and words on the next page.

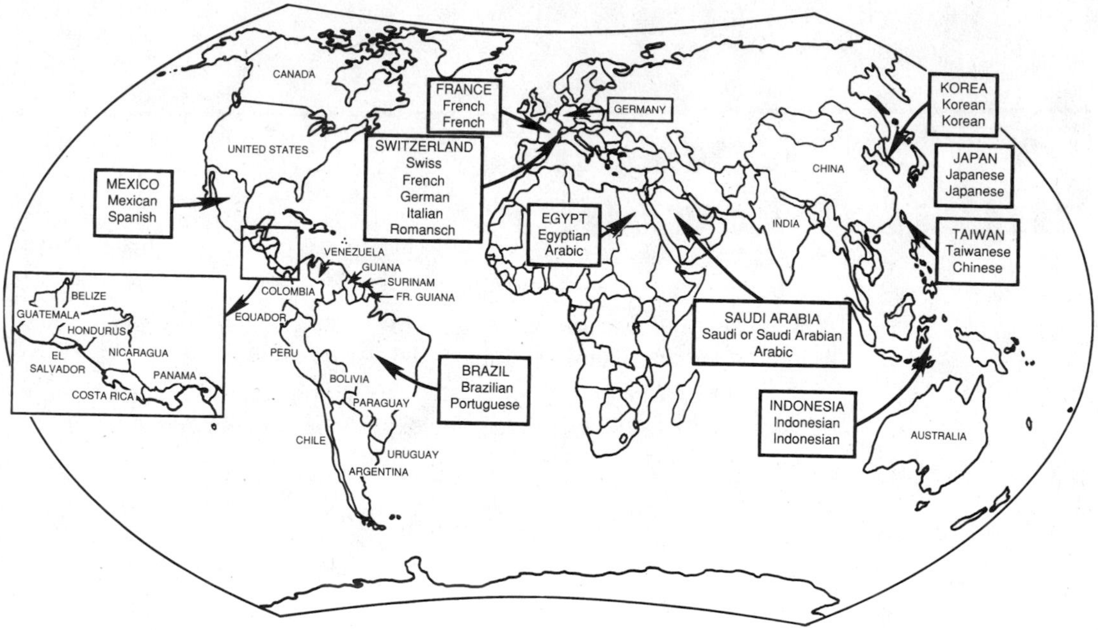

COUNTRY	NATIONALITY	LANGUAGE
Brazil	Brazilian	Portuguese
Egypt	Egyptian	Arabic
France	French	French
Indonesia	Indonesian	Indonesian
Japan	Japanese	Japanese
Korea	Korean	Korean
Mexico	Mexican	Spanish
Saudi Arabia	Saudi Saudi Arabian	Arabic
Switzerland	Swiss	French, German Italian, Romansch
Taiwan	Taiwanese	Chinese

A Communicative Grammar

interactions access

CHAPTER

Neighborhoods, Cities, and Towns

in this chapter

The Verb *Be* and Related Structures

Topic One: Affirmative Statements; Contractions; Questions

Topic Two: Nouns; Spelling Rules; Negative Statements; Possessive Adjectives

Topic Three: The Verb *Be* with Time and Weather

Topic Four: *There is / are;* Prepositions of Place; *at* and *at the* with Locations

TOPIC one

Affirmative Statements; Contractions; Questions

Setting the Context

prereading questions

Look at the picture. Where is the young woman? Is she happy?

Lost in New York City!

Hi! I'm Mariko. I'm from Japan. I'm Japanese. I'm an exchange student in San Diego. Right now I'm in New York on a special tour. My tour group is at the United Nations building. But where is the United Nations building? I'm lost! New York is a very big city. I'm confused, and I'm nervous. Where are my friends?

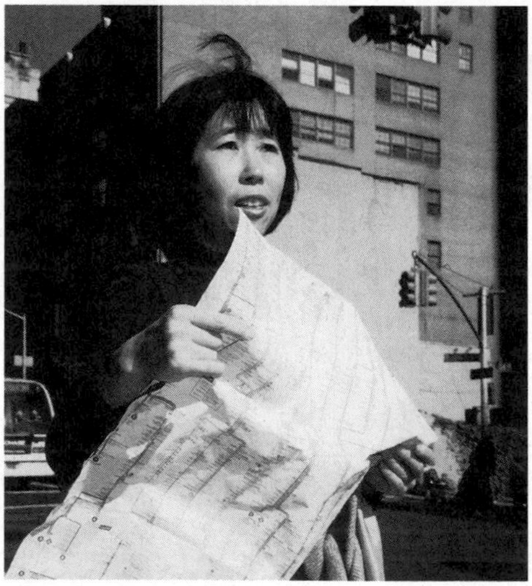

discussion questions

Circle T (True) or F (False).

example: T (F) Her name is Tomoko.

1. T F Mariko is from Japan.
2. T F Mariko is in San Diego right now.
3. T F Mariko is a business woman
4. T F Mariko is lost.

A Affirmative Statements

Subject* + Be + *adjective, noun, or phrase

singular	**plural**
I **am** Japanese.	We **are** Japanese.
You **are** students	You **are** students.
He / She / It **is** in New York.	They **are** in New York.

expressions	**examples**
be from (place)	I **am from** New York. She **is from** Athens.
be in (place)	We **are in** California now. They **are in** the library.

exercise 1

Use *am, is,* or *are* to complete this reading.

I _am_ Mariko, and I _____(1) an exchange student in San Diego. This week I _____(2) in New York. I _____(3) on a trip with people from my school. Today my friends and I _____(4) on a city tour. My friends _____(5) from many places. Anne _____(6) French. She _____(7) from Paris. Hassan _____(8) from Syria, and Carlos and Gabriel _____(9) from Mexico. We _____(10) excited but nervous! New York _____(11) very large, and it _____(12) crowded.

exercise 2

Use *is* or *are* and a nationality to complete these sentences.

1. Mariko _is_ from Japan. She _is_ _Japanese_.
2. Carlos _____ from Mexico. He _____ ___________.
3. Mr. Kim and Mr. Park _________ from Korea. They _____ ___________.
4. Anne and Chantal _____ from France. They _____ ___________.
5. Hassan _____ from Syria. He _____ ___________.
6. Benny _____ from Indonesia. He _____ ___________.
7. Gunter and Elizabeth _____ from Germany. They _____ ___________.

exercise 3 Use the verb *be* and *she, he* or *they* to complete these sentences.

1. Mariko _is_ from Japan. _She_ _is_ Japanese.
2. Elizabeth _____ from Germany. _____ _____ German.
3. Benny _____ from Indonesia. _____ _____ Indonesian.
4. Carlos and Gabriel are from Mexico. _____ _____ Mexican.
5. Anne is from France. _____ _____ French.
6. Mr. Park _____ from Korea. _____ _____ Korean.
7. Hassan and Ali _____ from Syria. _____ _____ Syrian.

exercise 4 Use *I* or *we* to complete this conversation.

LUCY: Good morning, everyone. _I_ am Lucy Moore _____ (1) am from New York. _____ (2) am happy to welcome you to my city.

BRUCE: Hi. _____ (3) am Bruce Moore. _____ (4) am from California, but New York is my city now! _____ (5) are your tour guides, and _____ (6) are very happy to be here today.

LUCY: _____ (7) are ready to start. Today _____ (8) are in Manhattan, the heart of New York City.

B Contractions

singular	plural	long form	
I'**m** from Spain.	We'**re** from Spain.	I **am**	We **are**
You'**re** from Korea.	You'**re** from Korea.	You **are**	You **are**
He'**s** / She'**s** / It'**s** } from Brazil.	They'**re** from Brazil.	He **is** / She **is** / It'**s** }	They **are**

Note: People often use contractions in conversation. Contractions are sometimes used with names: *Anne's from France; Hassan's from Syria.*

exercise 5 Read this paragraph. Then write it again with contractions.

example: Hi! I'm Carlos. . .

Hi! I am Carlos, and I am from Mexico. I am a student in Chicago, but I am in New York on a tour. My brother Gabriel is here in New York too. He is on vacation. We are very excited about our trip. New York is wonderful! It is big, crowded, and interesting. Some people on our tour are afraid of the city. They are nervous—especially Mariko. She is very nice, but she is always lost and confused. Not Gabriel and me! We are in love with New York!

C Yes/No Questions

Be + *subject* + *adjective, noun, or phrase*

singular	plural
Am I excited?	**Are** we excited?
Are you nervous?	**Are** you nervous?
Is {he / she / it} lost?	**Are** they lost?

exercise 6 Work with a partner. Ask and answer these questions. Answer using Yes or No.

example: A. **Is Mariko Japanese?**
B. **Yes.**
A. **Is Carlos Japanese?**
B. **No.**

1. Is Mariko in New York City now?
2. Is she from Hong Kong?
3. Is she an exchange student?
4. Are Carlos and Gabriel from Argentina?
5. Is Gabriel on vacation?
6. Are Carlos and Gabriel in love with New York City?
7. Are you from Japan?
8. Are you in New York now?

D Questions with *How, Where,* and *Who*

Question Word + Be + *Subject*

	questions	possible answers
How Greetings Age	 **How** are you? **How old** is he?	 Fine, thank you. Twenty-five.
Where Hometown or country Location	 **Where** are you from? **Where** are you?	 I am from Turkey. I'm in New York.
Who Identity	 **Who** is your roommate?	 My roommate is Mariko.

exercise 7

Write a question for each answer. Use *How, Where,* and *Who* in your questions. Then work with a partner. Take turns asking and answering the questions. The first one is done as an example.

1. *How are you* ____________?
   I'm fine, thanks, but I'm a little homesick.
2. ____________________?
   I'm from France.
3. ____________________?
   I'm twenty-five.
4. ____________________?
   My friend is Chantal.
5. ____________________?
   She's from France too.
6. ____________________?
   She's at the hotel right now.

E The Verb *Be* with Adjectives

Subject* + Be + *Adjective

singular	plural
I**'m tired.**	We**'re tired.**
You**'re happy.**	You**'re happy.**
He**'s** / She**'s** / It**'s** } **lost?**	They**'re lost?**

expressions	examples
be new here	**I am new here.**
be new to (place)	They **are new to** New York.

exercise 8

There are good things and bad things about New York City. Make sentences about the city. Use the pictures and the vocabulary to help you. Make one sentence for each adjective.

example: **Parts of New York City are beautiful.**

1. Parts of New York City are _____.
beautiful
√ clean
safe

2. Parts of New York City are _____.
ugly
dirty
dangerous

3. Buildings in New York City are _____.
large
modern

4. Buildings in New York City are _____.
small
old

5. New York City is _____.
crowded
noisy

6. New York City is _____.
peaceful
clean

7. Some New Yorkers are _____.
poor
unhappy
unfriendly
upset

8. Some New Yorkers are _____.
rich
happy
friendly
relaxed

exercise 9 Choose a word to describe these people.

bored	√homesick	thirsty
excited	hungry	tired

example:

1. Anne and Chantal are
homesick.

2. Mr. Park and Mr. Kim are
__________________.

3. Benny is

_____.

4. Carlos and Gabriel are

_____________________.

5. Hassan is

________.

6. Gunter and Elizabeth are

______________________.

F. Questions with *What and What . . . Like*

What + Be + *Subject*

	questions	possible answers
Names	**What** is your (first) name?	Mariko.
	What is your last (family) name?	It's Kanno.
Languages	**What** is your first (native) language?	Japanese.

What + Be + *Subject* + Like

Descriptions	**What** is Mariko **like?**	She's nice.
	What is New York **like**?	It's big and crowded.

exercise 10 Work with a partner. Ask and answer questions with *What . . . like?* Use the cues to talk about these cities.

example: Tokyo / big and crowded

A. **What is Tokyo like?**
B. **It's big and crowded.**

1. New York / large and very busy
2. San Francisco / beautiful
3. Cairo / crowded but very interesting
4. Los Angeles / modern but polluted
5. Rome / old and beautiful but very expensive
6. Minneapolis / safe and clean
7. Rio de Janeiro / fun
8. Paris / beautiful and interesting

Using What You've Learned

activity 1 **Introducing Your Classmates.** Who are all the students in your class? Can you remember? Go around the room in a chain. One by one, tell a student's name, country, and nationality. Your teacher will start.

example: TEACHER: **Mariko is from Japan. She is Japanese.**
MARIKO: **Carlos is from Mexico. He is Mexican.**
CARLOS: **Hassan . . .**

activity 2 **Telling About Yourself.** Use the paragraph in exercise 5 as a model. Write a paragraph about yourself, your city, and your friends or classmates.

activity 3 **Telling Stories.** Change your name. Change your age. Create a new person! Write your new name, age, country, and language on a piece of paper.

GROUP ACTIVITY

example: **Stella Blanco, 28, Argentina, Spanish**
or
William Shakespeare, 200+, England, English

Then work in small groups. Ask other students questions, and write the information in a chart like the one below. Here are some questions: Who are you? How old are you? Where are you from? What is your native language? Finally, introduce your "new" friends.

example: **This is my "new" friend, Stella Blanco. She is twenty-eight years old. She is from Argentina, and she speaks Spanish.**

name	age	country	language
Stella Blanco	28	Argentina	Spanish
William Shakespeare	200+	England	English

activity 4 **Learning About Students in Your Class.** In pairs or small groups, ask and answer questions about your hometowns. Write your information on the chart. Then take turns telling the class about the other students. Some questions:

- Where are you from?
- What is your hometown?
- What is your hometown like?
- Is it safe (dangerous, clean, dirty, etc.)?

name	hometown and country	description of hometown

example: **George is from Syria. His hometown is Damascus. Damascus . . .**

TOPIC **two**

Nouns; Spelling Rules; Negative Statements; Possessive Adjectives

Setting the Context

prereading questions

Look at this picture. Where are these people? Is their home near a large city?

Life in a Small Town

My name is Gary, and I'm a farmer. My hometown is Belleville, Wisconsin. It's a small town with a popular of about 1,800. It's not a busy, crowded place. It's very quiet and peaceful. The streets are safe, and the people are friendly. It's not dangerous here. Our air is not polluted. It's very clean. I'm happy in Belleville, and my family is very happy here too. Our dream is a good future in Belleville.

discussion questions

Complete these sentences.

1. His name is __________________.
2. He is a __________________.
3. Belleville is a __________________ town.
4. Gary and his family are __________________ in Belleville.

In 1900, about 10 million people in the United States lived on farms. Today, only about 4 million people live on farms. Is this the same or different in your home country? Why?

A. Nouns

	consonant sound	vowel sound	notes
Singular	I am **a doctor.** Are you **a student?** Bernardo is **a citizen.**	I am **an engineer.** Are you **an exchange student?** Bernardo is **an immigrant.**	Use *a* or *an* with a singular noun. Use *a* before a consonant sound. Use *an* before a vowel sound.
Plural	We are **doctors.** Are you **students?** They are **citizens.**	We are **engineers.** Are you **exchange students?** They are **immigrants.**	Do not use *a* or *an* with plural nouns.

exercise 1 Here are names of some occupations. Number them in alphabetical (A, B, C, . . .) order. Then add *a* or *an* before each occupation.

____ ____ nurse's aide	____ ____ musician
____ ____ plumber	____ ____ dentist
1 an airplane pilot	____ ____ student
____ ____ computer programmer	____ ____ engineer
____ ____ nurse	____ ____ bus driver
____ ____ carpenter	____ ____ secretary
____ ____ English teacher	____ ____ doctor
____ ____ businesswoman	____ ____ auto mechanic

exercise 2 Talk about these people. Follow the examples and make complete sentences. Add *a* or *an* when necessary.

examples:

Hau
Vietnam
musician

Hau is from Vietnam.
He is a musician.

Ali and
Mohammed
Jordan
carpenters

Ali and Mohammed are from Jordan.
They are carpenters.

1.

Soo Young
Korea
student

2.

Alfonso
Colombia
engineer

3.

Andrea
Argentina
doctor

4.

Nancy
the United States
flight attendant

5.

Centa and Werner
Switzerland
teachers

6.

Tomoko and Akiko
Japan
computer
programmers

7.

Isabelle and Pierre
France
factory workers

8.

Daniel and Ben
Hong Kong
auto mechanics

B. Spelling Rules for Nouns

	singular	plural
Most plural nouns end in *-s*.	friend student teacher	friends students teachers
Nouns with consonant + *y* change to *-ies*.	city family party	cities families parties
Nouns with vowel + *y* add *-s* only.	boy key play	boys keys plays
Nouns with *ch, sh, s,* and *x* add *-es*.	church dish kiss box	churches dishes kisses boxes
Nouns with consonant + *o* add *-es*.	potato tomato	potatoes tomatoes
Nouns with vowel + *o* add *-s* only.	radio zoo	radios zoos
Nouns with *f* or *fe* change to *-ves*.	shelf wife	shelves wives

some irregular nouns

person	people	foot	feet
child	children	goose	geese
man	men	mouse	mice
woman	women		

exercise 3

Write the plurals of these nouns.

example: child *children* dish *dishes*

1. man	__________	**6.** potato	__________
2. woman	__________	**7.** toy	__________
3. baby	__________	**8.** farm	__________
4. boy	__________	**9.** city	__________
5. church	__________	**10.** wife	__________

exercise 4

Use plural nouns to complete the reading.

Our *farms* (farm) are busy ___1___ (place). There are many ___2___ (animal) to take care of. We have ___3___ (cow), ___4___ (horse), ___5___ (Chicken), ___6___ (duck), and ___7___ (goose). Our ___8___ (child) have many ___9___ (pet): ___10___ (dog), ___11___ (cat), and even ___12___ (mouse)! Both our ___13___ (wife) have big ___14___ (garden) too. There are ___15___ (flower) and ___16___ (vegetable) to take care of. Right now we have ___17___ (carrot), ___18___ (onion), ___19___ (tomato), and ___20___ (potato). There are many, many ___21___ (thing) to do. Our ___22___ (family) are always busy on the farm.

Wheat, apples, and corn are three important products of U.S. farms. What are three important farm products in your home country?

C. Negative Statements

***Subject* + Be + not**

	long form	contraction
I **am not** late.	I'**m not** late.	
You **are not** late.	You'**re not** late.	
He / She / It **is not** late.	He'**s** / She'**s** / It'**s** **not** late.	He / She / It **isn't** late.
We / You / They **are not** late.	We'**re** / You'**re** / They'**re** **not** late.	We / You / They **aren't** late.

exercise 5 Complete these sentences with negative forms of the verb *be*. Use contractions.

1. The buses here ___aren't___ fast. In fact, they're very slow.
2. My town ______________ large. In fact, it's very small.
3. My town ______________ ugly. In fact, it's very pretty.
4. My neighborhood ______________ dangerous. In fact, it's very safe.
5. Our neighbors ______________ shy people. In fact, they're very friendly.
6. I ______________ bored here. In fact, I'm very happy.
7. You ______________ a stranger here. In fact, you're a part of the family!

exercise 6 These sentences are *not* true. To make them true, change them to the negative. Give all possible forms.

example: Denver is a small city.
Denver is not a small city.
Denver's not a small city.
Denver isn't a small city.

1. Gary is a businessman.
2. He's from a large city.
3. The White House is in New York.
4. It's near the United Nations building.
5. New York is a quiet city.
6. It is near Los Angeles.
7. You are from England.
8. I am tired of grammar.

exercise 7 Use *am, is,* or *are* to complete these sentences. Use a contraction form when possible. Use negative forms when you see *(not)*.

1. I'm________ from Victoria, British Columbia. It ____1____ (not) a big city, but it ____2____ (not) a small town either. It ____3____ (not on the mainland. It ____4____ on Vancouver Island. Victoria ____5____ very beautiful. The weather ____6____ often warm and sunny, but it ____7____ sometimes rainy.

2. We ____1____ from Marlboro, Vermont, and we ____2____ very happy here. Marlboro ____3____ (not) very big, so it ____4____ (not) noisy or crowded. Our streets ____5____ (not) dangerous or dirty. Our neighbors ____6____ friendly, and our little town ____7____ very nice.

3. Hi! My name ____1____ Natalie. I ____2____ twenty-two. I ____3____ from Switzerland, but I ____4____ (not) there now. I ____5____ in Houston. Houston ____6____ huge. It ____7____ (not) a quiet city, but it ____8____ interesting.

D. Possessive Adjectives

Singular	I am Natalie. You are Nancy. He is Hau. She is Mei. It is Lukas. (the dog)	**My** name is Natalie. **Your** name is Nancy. **His** name is Hau. **Her** name is Mei. **Its** name is Lukas.
Plural	We are Ali and Mohammed. You are Isabelle and Pierre. They are Daniel and Ben.	**Our** names are Ali and Mohammed. **Your** names are Isabelle and Pierre. **Their** names are Daniel and Ben.

exercise 8 Circle the correct form.

1. (I / My) name is Natalie.
2. (I / My) am from Switzerland.
3. (We / Our) hometown is Berne.
4. (We / Our) are from Switzerland.
5. (I / My) family is in Switzerland now.
6. What is (you / your) name?
7. How old are (you / your)?
8. (He / His) name is Gary.
9. (She / Her) is Nancy.
10. (They / Their) dog is Lukas.
11. (It / Its) name is Lukas.
12. (It / Its) is seven years old.

exercise 9 Use *I, we, my,* or *our* to complete these sentences.

1. We are from Big City, U.S.A. _______ (1) city is very crowded. _______ (2) are is polluted, and _______ (3) streets are dirty and dangerous. _______ (4) lives are not easy here. _______ (5) aren't very happy in Big City. _______ (6) dream is a home in the country.

2. _______ (1) am from Middletown, Canada. _______ (2) city isn't big, but it isn't small either. _______ (3) life is peaceful and _______ (4) am very happy. _______ (5) neighbors are friendly, and _______ (6) neighborhood is safe.

exercise 10 Use *he, she, they, his, her,* or *their* to complete this reading.

Isabelle and Pierre are from France. They are factory workers. _______ (1) jobs aren't very interesting, and _______ (2) are often difficult. Isabelle's work is sometimes dangerous. _______ (3) isn't happy with _______ (4) job, and _______ (5) dream is to study at the university someday. Pierre is happy with _______ (6) job, but _______ (7) is worried about Isabelle. _______ (8) dream is to save money for Isabelle's education.

Using What You've Learned

activity 1

Telling Stories. Write a story about a friend or a relative. Use these questions and ideas from exercises 9 and 10 to help you.

1. Who is this person?
2. Where is he or she from?
3. What is that place like?
4. What is the person's occupation?
5. Is he or she happy?
6. What are that person's dreams for the future?

TOPIC three

The Verb Be with Time and Weather

Setting the Context

prereading questions

Who is the woman in this picture? Is the weather nice today?

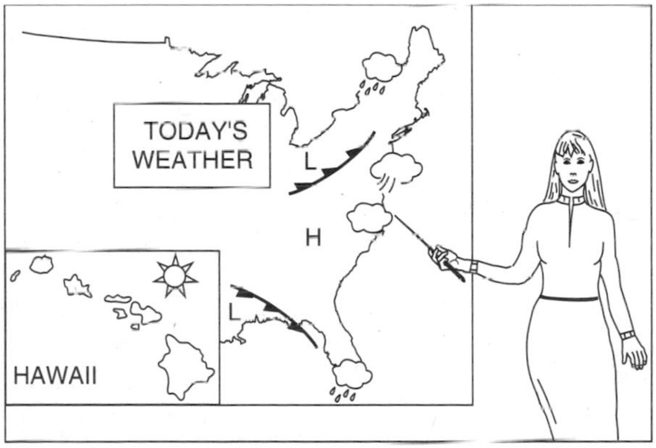

"Good evening. Today is March 24, and the weather is bad on the East Coast. Everywhere it's rainy, snowy, foggy, cloudy, or windy! Right now, at 6:15, it's rainy in Miami. It's foggy in Washington, D.C., and the airport is closed. It's cold and windy in New York City. In Montreal, it's snowy. The place to be right now is Hawaii!"

discussion questions

Complete these sentences.

1. It's March ______________________________.
2. In Miami, it's ______________________________.
3. In Washington, it's ______________________________.
4. The airport is ______________________________.
5. In Montreal, it's ______________________________.

A. Using *It* with Weather

What + Be + *Subject* (+ Like) **questions**	**It + Be + *Adjective*** **possible answers**
What's the weather today?	**It's** beautiful.
What's the weather **like**?	**It's** terrible.
What's it **like** out(side)?	**It's** nice.

exercise 1 Make complete sentences about the weather in these cities. Use the weather maps to help you. Use the map on the left to answer questions 1–5 and the map on the right to answer questions 6–10.

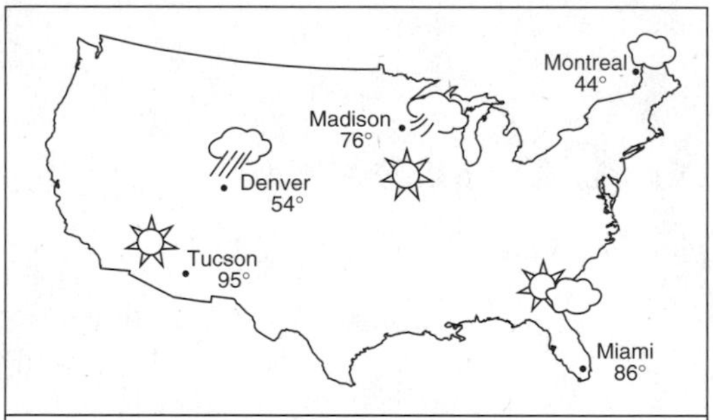

September 21 — The First Day of Fall

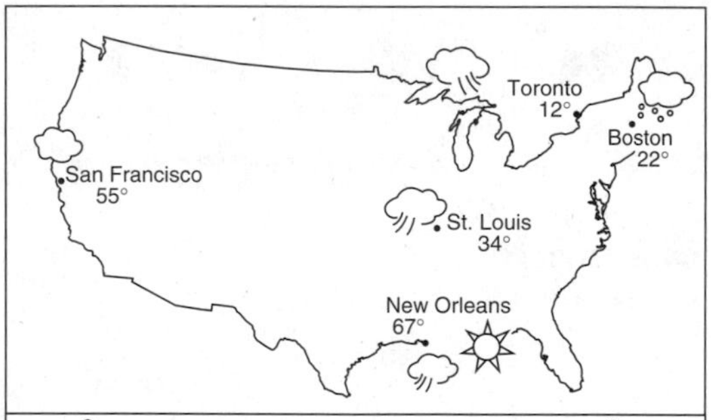

February 14 — Valentine's Day

example: New York / cloudy and cool
New York is cloudy and cool today.

1. Madison, Wisconsin / sunny, breezy, and warm
2. Denver, Colorado / cloudy, rainy, and cool
3. Miami, Florida / hot and humid
4. Montreal, Quebec / cold and cloudy
5. Tucson, Arizona / very hot and dry
6. Boston, Massachusetts / cold and snowy
7. New Orleans, Louisiana / warm and breezy
8. St. Louis, Missouri / cold and rainy
9. San Francisco, California / foggy and cool
10. Toronto, Ontario / very cold and windy

CULTURE NOTE

Many North Americans talk about the weather to start a conversation. For example, they say, "Nice day, isn't it?" Or "Hot enough for you?" Or "It's very cold for this time of year." Do people talk about the weather in your home country? How do they start a conversation?

B. Using *It* with Time

What (+ *Noun*)+ Be + It questions	**It + Be + *Time Expression*** possible answers
What time is it?	It's eight o'clock.
	It's 8:20 P.M.
What day is it?	It's Friday.
What month is it?	It's August.
What day is it?	It's August 20th.
What's the date (today)?	It's ______.
What year is it?	It's 19______.

Note: 12:00 A.M. = midnight; 12:00 P.M. – noon. See Appendix Two (page 306 and 307) for a complete list of numbers, days, months, and seasons.

exercise 2 Tell the time, day, or date.

example: **Its's three o'clock.**

1.

2.

3.

4.

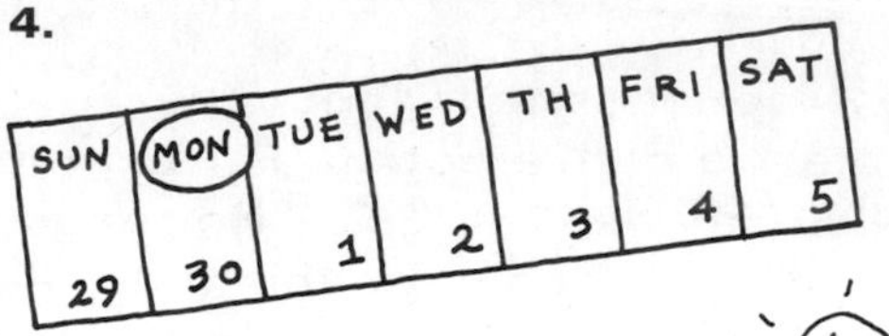

5.

6.

7. 8. 9.

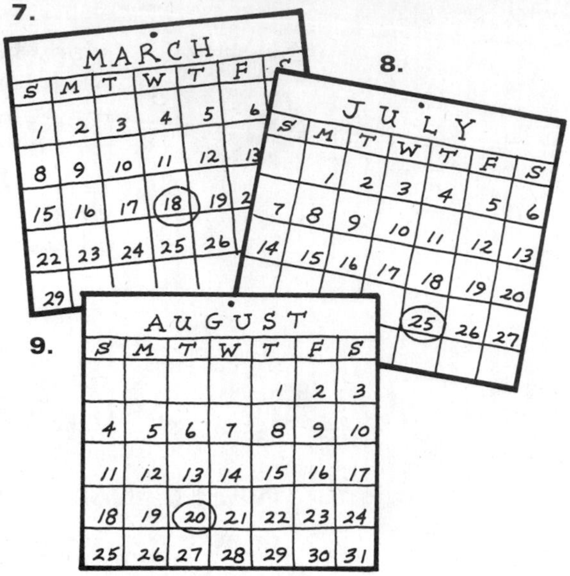

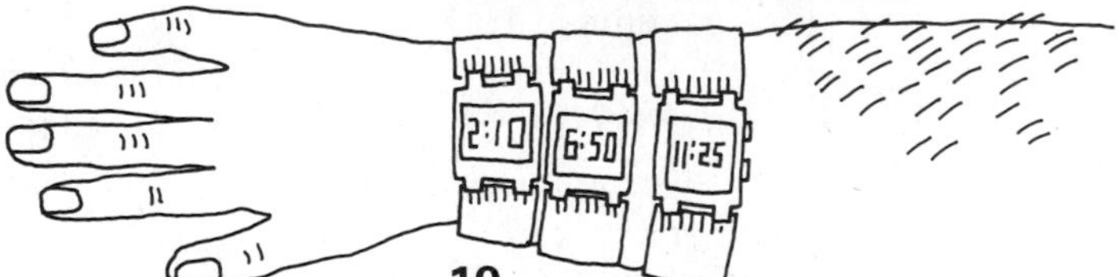

10. 11. 12.

exercise 3 Work with a partner. Ask and answer these questions.

1. What time is it right now?
2. What day is it?
3. What's the date today?
4. What month is it?
5. What season is it?
6. What year is it?

C. Prepositions of Time—*in, on, at, from . . . to (until)*

	period of time	***examples***
in		Alex was born **in** the afternoon or **in** the morning.
	Month	Alex was born **in** July.
	Season	Alex was born **in** the summer.
	Year	Alex was born **in** 1986.
on	Days	My birthday is **on** Saturday.
	Dates	My birthday is **on** September 20th.
	Exceptions: *Weekdays*	I go to school **on** weekdays.
	Weekends	I'm at home **on** weekends.
at	Specific times	My birthday party is **at** 8:30 P.M.
	Exception: *At Night*	The party is **at** night.
from . . . to (until)	Beginning and ending times	The dinner is **from** 6:00 **to** 8:00. The party is **from** 8:30 **until** midnight.

expressions with birthdays	***examples***
What (day) is your birthday?	It's (**on**) September 20th.
When were you born?	I was born **on** September 20th.

exercise 4 Use *on* or *at* to complete these sentences.

1. Martin was born _on_ August 20th. He was born _____ Friday _____ 8:20 P.M.
2. Marina's birthday is _____ December 23rd. She was born _____ night.
3. Gary's birthday is _____ April 26th. He was born _____ midnight.
4. Alex's birthday is _____ July 25th. He was born _____ Thursday _____ 5:25 P.M.
5. Jennifer's birthday is _____ November 27th. She was born _____ 6:30 P.M.

exercise 5 Circle the correct prepositions.

I'm usually awake (at / on) 6:15 A.M. (in / on)₁ weekdays. I'm at work (from / at)₂ 8:00 (in / on)₃ the morning. I work (at / from)₄ 8:00 (in / to)₅ 4:30 (at / in)₆ the afternoon. Then I'm at school (in / from)₇ 7:00 (on / to) 8:30 (at / in)₉ night. (In / On)₁₀ the weekends, I'm very lazy. I'm still in bed (at / from)₁₁ 10:00 A.M.

exercise 6 In pairs, talk about your usual schedules. Then write a short composition about yourself. Use the paragraph in exercise 5 as an example.

exercise 7 Use *in, on, from,* or *to* to complete this reading.

The weather in Wisconsin is very changeable. ___In___ the spring, it's cool and rainy. _______ (1) the summer, it's often very hot. _______ (2) the fall, the weather is lovely. Then, _______ (3) November _______ (4) April, it's cold and snowy. I'm always busy, good weather or bad weather. But _______ (5) Sundays, I rest a little.

exercise 8 Use *at, in, on, from,* or *to* to complete this reading.

My life in New York City is very busy. My home is far from my work, so ___from___ Monday _______ (1) Friday, I am awake _______ (2) 5:00 _______ (3) the morning. _______ (4) Monday, Wednesday, and Friday, I take the bus to work. _______ (5) Tuesday and Thursday, I drive my car. My day is very long. I am usually home _______ (6) 7:30 or 8:00 P.M. _______ (7) the weekend, I sleep late.

Using What You've Learned

activity 1 **Telling About the Weather.** Write two sentences about the weather in your city today. Then write two sentences about your hometown. What's the weather like there? If you are not sure, use *probably* in those sentences.

example: **Today it's sunny here. It's also windy and cool. In Bangkok, is't probably hot and humid. It's probably very cloudy.**

activity 2 **Telling Time.** What time is it right now in your hometown? What day is it? In small groups or as a class, talk about the times in different places and the calendars in different religions or cultures. Make a list for the entire class.

activity 3 **Telling About Birthdays.** As a class, take turns telling about your birthday. Give the date. If you know, also say the day of the week and the time of day. One student can write down all the birth dates.

TOPIC four

There is / are; *Prepositions of Place; at and at the with Locations*

Setting the Context

prereading questions This is a map of a region in the United States—New England. What states are in New England? What is the major city in New England?

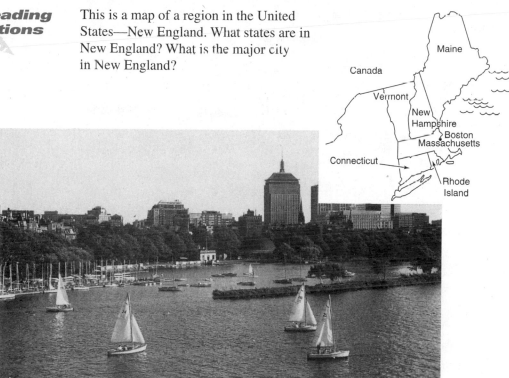

Boston

Boston is a beautiful city on the East Coast of the United States. It is the capital of Massachusetts, one of the states in New England. Boston is an old city, and there are many historic buildings, monuments, and churches. The State House (Massachusetts's capitol), Old City Hall, the King's Chapel, and Faneuil Hall are all downtown. Nearby there are also many interesting neighborhoods to visit, such as the North End, Beacon Hill, and Chinatown. Also, there are many lovely parks on the Charles River and along Boston Harbor.

Boston is an old, historic city in the United States. What is an historic place in your home country? What are some interesting things to see there?

discussion questions

Circle T (True) or F (False).

1. T F Boston is on the West Coast of the United States.
2. T F Boston is the capital of New Jersey.
3. T F There are many historic buildings in Boston.
4. T F There is a Chinese neighborhood in Boston.
5. T F There aren't many parks in Boston.

A. *There is / are*—Affirmative and Negative Statements

Affirmative Statements

There + be + *subject*

	Long Form	*Contraction*
With a singular noun	**There is** a museum downtown.	**There's** a museum downtown.
With plural nouns	**There are** many banks downtown.	**There're** many banks downtown.

Negative Statements

There + be + not + *subject*

	Long Form	*Contraction*
With a singular noun	**There is not** a post office nearby.	**There isn't** a post office nearby.
With plural nouns	**There are not** many stores downtown.	**There aren't** many stores downtown.

exercise 1

Use *is* or *are* to complete these sentences.

1. There ___is___ a subway in San Francisco.
2. There _______ many parks in San Francisco.
3. There ___are___ many hills in San Francisco.
4. There _______ many cable cars.
5. There _______ a wharf for boats called Fisherman's Wharf.
6. There _______ a large Chinese neighborhood in San Francisco.
7. There _______ a tower in San Francisco.
8. There _______ many bridges.

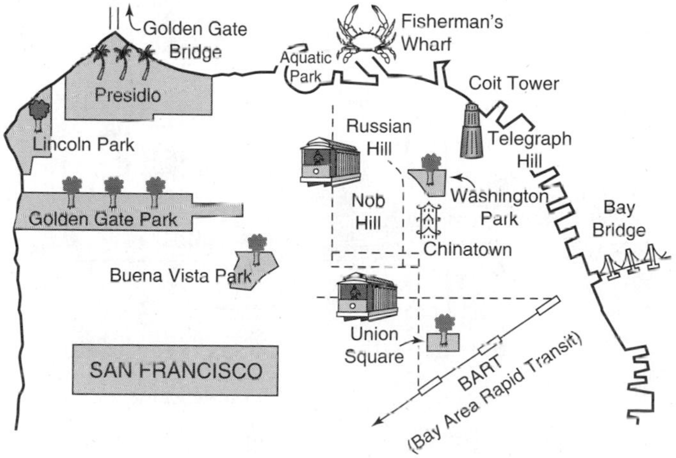

exercise 2 Use *isn't* or *aren't* to complete these sentences.

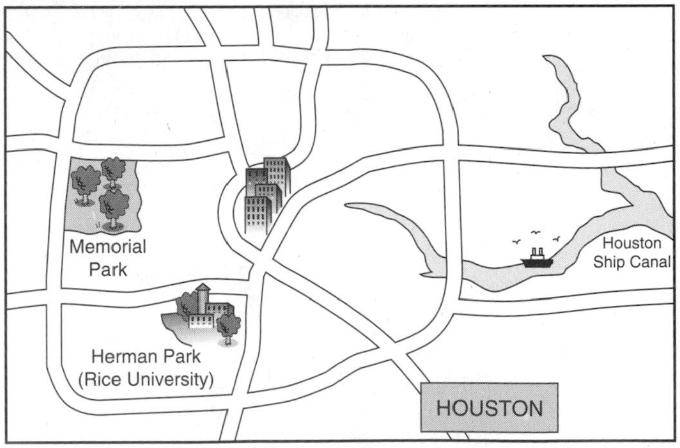

1. There isn't a wharf in Houston.
2. There aren't many large parks.
3. There _______ many rivers.
4. There _______ mountains nearby.
5. There _______ many hills in Houston.
6. There _______ any cable cars.
7. There _______ a subway.
8. There _______ any snow in Houston.

B. *There is / are*— Questions and Short Answers

Be + there + *subject*

	questions	possible answers	
		Affirmative	***Negative***
Singular	**Is there** a post office nearby?	Yes, **there is.**	No, **There isn't.**
Plural	**Are there** many stores downtown?	Yes, **there are.**	No, **There aren't.**

exercise 3 Ask and answer questions with a partner. Use the cues to make questions. Use the map to help you.

examples: many bridges to Manhattan

A. **Are there many bridges to Manhattan?**

B. **Yes, there are.**

an island in the East River

A. **Is there an island in the East River?**

B. **Yes, there is.**

1. a subway in Manhattan
2. many tunnels
3. four rivers around Manhattan
4. a bridge to the Statue of Liberty
5. many ferries to Manhattan
6. a train station in Manhattan
7. a large park
8. a zoo in Central Park
9. many museums in Manhattan
10. an airport in Manhattan
11. an airport in Brooklyn
12. an airport in Queens

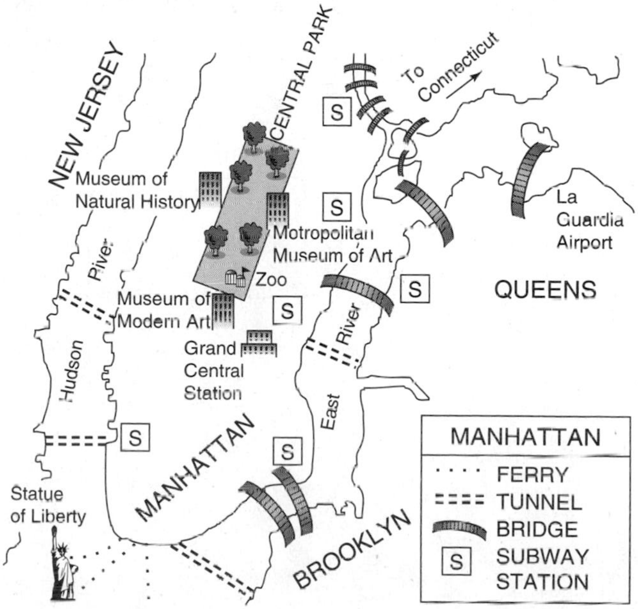

C. The Verb *Be* with Prepositions of Place—*in, on, at*

		examples
in	Buildings Cities States Regions Countries	She lives **in** an apartment. Her apartment is **in** Boston. Boston is **in** Massachusetts. Massachusetts is **in** New England. New England is **in** the United States.
on	Bodies of water and coasts (including the East Coast and the West Coast) Streets	Boston is **on** the Charles River. Massachusetts is **on** the East Coast. Her apartment is **on** Beacon Street.
at	Specific addresses and many specific locations	She lives **at** 121 Beacon Street. She works **at** the bank. Right now she is **at** the store. Her sister is **at** the library.

exercise 4 Complete these sentences with *at* or *on.*

1. The library is _on_ Second Avenue.
2. The library is _____ 413 Second Avenue.
3. Mariko is _____ the library now.
4. The post office is _____ the river.
5. It's _____ 2020 River Street.
6. Carlos is _____ the post office now.
7. Carlos's apartment is also _____ River Street.

exercise 5 Form sentences with *in* or *on*.

example: Miami / the U.S.A.

Miami is in the U.S.A.

1. Paris / France
2. Geneva / Switzerland
3. Tokyo / Japan
4. Chicago / Lake Michigan
5. San Francisco / the Pacific Ocean
6. Buenos Aires / Argentina
7. Miami / the Atlantic Ocean
8. Cairo / the Nile River

exercise 6 Are these sentences true? Which are false? Use negatives to correct the false sentences. Then tell the true location of each place.

examples: San Diego and San Francisco are in Oregon.

San Diego and San Francisco aren't in Oregon. They're in California.

1. Santa Barbara is in Oregon.
2. The Cascade Mountains are in Arizona.
3. Reno is on the Pacific Ocean.
4. Vancouver and Edmonton are in Washington.
5. Los Angeles is on the Pacific Ocean.
6. Seattle is on the Columbia River.
7. Phoenix and Tucson are in Nevada.
8. The Grand Canyon is in Arizona.

D. Using *at the* and *at* with Locations

At the and *at* are used with some locations. With other locations, *at the* and *at* are *not* used; only the place expression is used.

at the	at	no preposition or article
I am **at the bank.**	My sister is **at home.**	My brother is **there.**
at the bank	at church	downtown
at the beach	at class	(over) here
at the hospital	at home*	(over) there
at the library	at school	far away
at the movies	at work	nearby
at the museum		
at the post office		
at the store		

**Note:* People say both "He's at home" and "He's home."

exercise 7

In a chain, ask and answer questions with *Where.* Use the following cues and add two of your own. Continue until each student has a turn. Use the chart above to help you.

example: Ali / bank
George / school
A. **Where's Ali?**
B. **He's at the bank. Where's George?**
C. **He's at school. Where's . . .**

1. Anne / home
2. Carlos / downtown
3. Jack / museum
4. Fred / work
5. Jane / over there
6. Lucy / class
7. Rick / post office
8. Sandy / store
9. Mary / movies
10. Laura / church
11. /
12. /

exercise 8 Circle the correct words to complete this letter.

November 14

Dear Akiko,

Greetings from the United States! I am back (in / on) San Diego now. My apartment (is / are)[1] very small and expensive, but (it's / they're)[2] nice. My roommate (is / are)[3] friendly too! (She / Her)[4] name is Anne, and she (is / are)[5] from the United States.

(I / My)[6] life here (is / are)[7] very busy. I am (at / at the)[8] school every day. My classes are (in / on)[9] the afternoon and (in / at)[10] night. In the morning, I am usually (at / at the)[11] library. (There / They're)[12] is always a lot of homework!

(In / On)[13] the weekends, I[16] (am / are)[14] busy too. San Diego[17] (am / is)[15] beautiful, and (it's / its) very interesting. There (is / are) a wonderful zoo here, and there (is / are)[18] many parks. San Diego is (at / on)[19] the Pacific Ocean, and I think there (is / are)[20] thousands of boats in the harbor. (I / My)[21] am in love with the ocean!

The weather (in / on)[22] San Diego is usually very nice. (In / On)[23] the morning, it's sometimes foggy. Most of the time, it's (sun / sunny)[24] and dry.

It's time to study again. I miss you a lot! I'm homesick today, but I really (am / is)[25] happy here.

Love,

Mariko

Using What You've Learned

activity 1

Describing Places. In pairs, write sentences about your town or city. Try to write at least six sentences. Give both affirmative and negative sentences.

example: **There are buses here.**
There isn't a subway here.

activity 2

Describing Locations. Where is your house or apartment? Form groups of four and then separate into pairs. In each pair, tell each other your street name and then give your specific address. Remember the information; do not write it.

Then, in your group, change partners. Give your first partner's street name and specific address to your new partner. Your new partner must check the information with your first partner.

example:
A. **My apartment is on River Street. It's at 2020 River Street.**
B. **My house is on. . . . It's at . . .**
B. **Carlo's apartment is on River Street. It's at 2020 River Street.**
C. **Ali's apartment . . .**
C. **Carlos, your apartment is on River Street. It's at 2020 River Street.**
A. **Correct!**

activity 3

Writing Letters. Write a letter to someone who reads English. Use the letter in exercise 8 as an example. Tell about your life now—your studies, your apartment or home, and your city. Then mail your letter!

CHAPTER two

Shopping— A National Pastime?

in this chapter

The Present Continuous Tense and Related Structures

Topic One:	Affirmative Statements and Questions; *and; too*
Topic Two:	Spelling Rules; Negative Statements; *but*
Topic Three:	More Prepositions of Place; *there is / are* + verb + *-ing;* *It* versus *There*
Topic Four:	*Be going to; to* and *to the* with Locations; *because*

TOPIC one

Affirmative Statements and Questions; and; too

Setting the Context

prereading questions

In the picture on page 39, two friends are in a clothing store. What are they looking for?

SALESPERSON: Good morning. May I help you? Are you looking for something special?

GLORIA: Yes, very special. My friend is looking for a gift, and I'm shopping for clothes for a job interview. I'm looking for something serious, like a dark blue suit. Hmm . . . maybe a white blouse and a gray skirt. I'm trying to decide.

MIGUEL: I'm looking for a birthday gift for my mother. It's her birthday, and we're having a party tonight.

GLORIA: Miguel, how about a scarf or a purse? By the way, what time is the party tonight?

MIGUEL: It's right after dinner. Come at seven. Cristina is coming then, and Fernando is too.

discussion questions

1. Are Gloria and Miguel buying something special?
2. What kind of outfit is Gloria thinking about?
3. What is Miguel looking for?
4. Is Gloria going to the birthday party?

A. Affirmative Statements

Subject + *be* + verb + *-ing*

long form	contraction	notes
I **am working.**	I'**m working.**	The present continuous tense tells about actions in progress now. Common time expressions with this tense are *now* or *right now, today, this week, this month, this year,* and so on.
You **are working.**	You'**re working.**	
He / She / It } **is working.**	He'**s** / She'**s** / It'**s** } **working.**	
We / You / They } **are working.**	We'**re** / You'**re** / They'**re** } **working.**	

exercise 1 Underline all present continuous tense verbs in the conversation on page 38.

exercise 2 Use present continuous verbs and complete these sentences. Use the picture below and the verbs in parentheses for help.

1. Miguel is buying________ (buying) gifts.
2. The little boys ________________ (playing).
3. The little girl and her mother ________________ (taking) a walk.
4. They ________________ (looking) at toys.
5. The teenage girls ________________ (shopping) for new clothes.
6. The woman ________________ (going) home.
7. The teenage boy ________________ (listening) to music.
8. The old man ________________ (reading) the newspaper.

B. Yes/No Questions and Short Answers

Be* + subject + verb + *ing

questions	possible answers	
	AFFIRMATIVE	NEGATIVE
Are you **working?**	Yes, **I am.**	No, **I'm not.**
Is he / she / it **working?**	Yes, **he is.**	No, **he isn't.** No, **he's not.**
	Yes, **she is.**	No, **she isn't.** No, **she's not.**
	Yes, **it is.**	No, **it isn't.** No, **it's not.**
Are we **working?**	Yes, **we are.**	No, **we aren't.** No, **we're not.**
Are you **working?**	Yes, **we are.**	No, **we aren't.** No, **we're not.**
Are they **working?**	Yes, **they are.**	No, **they aren't.** No, **they're not.**

exercise 3

Work with a partner. Ask and answer these questions about the picture in exercise 2. One student asks the questions. The other student looks at the picture and gives a short answer.

example: A: **Is the woman carrying packages?**
B: **Yes, she is.**

1. Is Miguel buying gifts?
2. Is the old man reading a book?
3. Are the little boys playing?
4. Are the boys riding bicycles?
5. Is the teenage boy dancing?
6. Is he carrying a radio?
7. Is the little girl taking a walk with her father?

C. And

	examples	notes
Two Sentences	I'm looking for new clothes. My friend is shopping for a gift.	*And* means "also" or "in addition." It can join two sentences. Use a comma (,) before *and.*
One Sentence	I'm looking for new clothes, **and** my friend is shopping for a gift.	

exercise 4

Use *and* to join each pair of sentences. Remember to add a comma when you write each new sentence.

example: I'm looking for new shoes.
My sister is buying a new purse.
I'm looking for new shoes, and my sister is buying a new purse.

1. Gloria is looking for some new clothes.
The salesperson is helping her.
2. Cristina is buying a gift.
Fernando is looking for a birthday card.
3. Mrs. Gómez is having a birthday.
Miguel is planning a party for her.
4. We're going to a restaurant tonight.
Our teacher is paying for the dinner.
5. I'm ______________ after class.
My friends are ______________ .
6. I'm ______________ this weekend.
My friends are ______________ .

D. *Too* with Short Statements

long form	short form	notes
I'm spending a lot of money. My brother is spending a lot of money.	I'm spending a lot of money, **and** my brother **is too.**	*Too* means "also" in affirmative statements. Do not use contractions in these statements.
My brother is spending a lot of money. I'm spending a lot of money.	My brother is spending a lot of money, **and** I **am too.**	

exercise 5 Complete these sentences with a form of the verb *be* and the word *too.*

1. I'm looking for something special, and my friend ___is___ ___too___.
2. Cristina is going to the birthday party, and Fernando ________ ________.
3. Miguel is buying a gift, and I ________ ________.
4. I'm spending a lot of money, and you ________ ________.
5. Gloria is looking for a job, and I ________ ________.
6. Ann is working at the mall, and my roommates ________ ________.
7. John is playing tennis this afternoon, and Miki ________ ________.
8. Jeff is watching television, and Jack ________ ________.
9. I'm studying English very hard, and my classmates ________ ________.

E. Information Questions with *What*

What + be + subject + verb + -ing

statement	information question
She's buying a sweater. They are playing.	**What** is she buying? **What** are they doing?

exercise 6 What are these people doing? With a partner, ask and answer questions about the people.

examples: A: **What is the little boy doing?**
B: **He's playing.**

B: **What are the little girls doing?**
A: **They're riding bicycles.**

1\.

2\.

3\.

4\.

5\.

6\.

exercise 7 Work with a partner. Ask and answer questions about the picture. Use the verbs below and make questions with *what.* Make at least six questions.

example: A: **What are the little girls wearing?**
B: **They're wearing jackets and mittens.**

carrying	eating	riding
doing	reading	√ wearing
drinking		

F. Descriptions—Questions with *What* + Noun

What + noun is used to ask for specific information. Many different nouns can be used in these questions. Compare the forms:

question word	form
what	**What** + **be** + subject + verb + **-ing**
what kind (of)	**What kind** (+ **of** + noun) + **be** + subject + verb + **-ing**
what + noun	**What** + noun + **be** + subject + verb + **-ing**

	questions	possible answers
what	**What** are you looking for?	A sweater.
what kind (of)	**What kind of sweater** are you looking for?	A wool sweater.
	What kind are you looking for?	
	What color are you looking for?	Red.
what + noun	**What size** are you looking for?	Medium.

exercise 8

Read this dialogue. Then use the vocabulary on page 47 to create three different dialogues. Choose one dialogue and role-play it with a partner. Ask your teacher for help with new vocabulary.

example:

SALESPERSON: May I help you?

GLORIA: I'm looking for something __serious__. I'm buying __clothes__ for __an interview__.

SALESPERSON: What __color__ are you looking for?

GLORIA: __Dark blue or dark gray__.

SALESPERSON: How about this?

VOCABULARY

casual	clothes	a birthday	color	light blue
elegant	a coat	an interview		dark blue
inexpensive	a gift	a party		red
nice	shoes	school		white, etc.
serious	a suit	a trip	size	small
special	a sweater	a wedding		medium
warm		work		large
				size 12, size 36, etc.

1. May I help you?

   I'm looking for something __________ .

   I'm buying __________ for __________ .

   What __________ are you looking for?

   __________ .

   How about this?

2. May I help you?

   I'm looking for something __________ .

   I'm buying __________ for __________ .

   What __________ are you looking for?

   ______________________________ .

   How about this?

3. May I help you?

   I'm looking for something __________ . I'm buying __________ for __________ .

   What __________ are you looking for?

   ______________________________ .

   How about this?

In stores, sales people ask "May I help you?" or "Are you looking for something special?" If you aren't, you can say, "No thank you. I'm just looking" or "Just looking, thank you."

Using What You've Learned

activity 1

Describing People. In pairs or small groups, look at the picture in exercise 7. Tell a story about one or more of the people. For example, who is the woman in the picture? What is she carrying? Where is she going? What is she thinking about?

activity 2

Describing People. Write your name on a piece of paper. Your teacher will collect all the names and put them in a bag. Then choose a name, but do not say it. What is that person wearing? Describe the person's clothing, but do not tell the person's name. Other students guess the name.

example:

A: **This student is wearing a white sweater, blue jeans, leather boots, and one gold earring.**

B: **It's Anna!**

C: **No, it isn't. It's Antonio.**

activity 3

Telling Stories. This is a picture of a birthday party. Create a story about it. Who is at the party? What is everyone doing? In pairs or small groups, tell a story about the party.

TOPIC two

Spelling Rules; Negative Statements; Using but

Setting the Context

prereading questions

In this picture, two friends are talking about money. Are they rich? What are they thinking about?

MICHELLE: Are you buying a new coat this winter?

DONNA: No, I'm not spending money on clothes, and my husband isn't either.

MICHELLE: Why? Are you saving money?

DONNA: Yes. Peter and I are saving money for a new car. We're not going to the movies, and we're not eating in restaurants.

MICHELLE: What kind of car are you looking for?

DONNA: We're looking for a small car with good gas mileage. We're not buying a big car again! It's too expensive.

MICHELLE: I'm not saving! I'm spending *all* my money on new clothes.

discussion questions

1. Is Donna buying a new coat this winter?
2. Are Donna and Peter eating in restaurants often?
3. Is Michelle saving for a new car?
4. Are Donna and Peter buying a big new car?

A. Spelling Rules with *-ing*

ending		*-ing* spelling	
Consonant and *-e*		Drop the *-e* and add *-ing.*	
drive	use	driving	using
make	write	making	writing
One vowel and one consonant (one-syllable words)		Double the final consonant and add *-ing.*	
get	sit	getting	sitting
shop	run	shopping	running
Other endings		Add *-ing.*	
buy	snow	buying	snowing
fix	study	fixing	studying
look	try	looking	trying
pay	work	paying	working
rest		resting	

exercise 1 Underline all present continuous verbs in the conversation on page 49.

exercise 2 Give the spellings of the *-ing* forms.

1. sit sitting
2. shop ________
3. study ________
4. buy ________
5. rest ________
6. make ________
7. use ________
8. run ________
9. pay ________
10. take ________
11. eat ________
12. sleep ________
13. get ________
14. drive ________

exercise 3 Use the present continuous tense to complete these sentences.

1. Donna ___is buying___ (buy) a gift.
2. She ____________ (write) a check. She ____________ (use) a pen.
3. Peter ____________ (make) a list.
4. She ____________ (draw) a picture, and he ____________ (cut) some paper.
5. He ____________ (sleep).
6. She ____________ (study).
7. He ____________ (look) out the window.
8. She ____________ (ride) a bicycle. Her dog ____________ (run) after the bicycle.
9. She ____________ (sit) on the sofa. She ____________ (watch) TV.

B. Negative Statements

Subject + *be* + *not* + verb + *-ing*

long form	contraction	
I **am not working.**	I'**m not working.**	
You **are not working.**	You'**re not working.**	You **aren't working.**
He / She / It } **is not working.**	He'**s** / She'**s** / It'**s** } **not working.**	He / She / It } **isn't working.**
We / You / They } **are not working.**	We'**re** / You'**re** / They'**re** } **not working.**	We / You / They } **aren't working.**

exercise 4 These sentences have negative contractions. Give the other form of each negative contraction.

example: We're not spending money.
We aren't spending money.

1. She's not buying new clothes.
2. He isn't using a credit card.
3. They're not spending money.
4. We're not eating in restaurants.
5. It's not working.
6. You aren't driving the car often.

exercise 5 Make negative sentences from these cues. Use the contraction *they're*.

example: not spend a lot of money these days
They're not spending a lot of money these days.

1. not eat in restaurants
2. not drive the car very often
3. not buy new clothes
4. not make long-distance phone calls
5. not go to movies
6. not use credit cards

C. *But*

	examples	notes
Two Sentences	I am buying a tie. My friend is just looking.	*But* shows a difference or contrast. It can join two sentences. Use a comma (,) before *but.*
One Sentence	I am buying a tie, **but** my friend is just looking.	

exercise 6

Use *but* to join each pair of sentences. Remember to add a comma when you write each new sentence.

example: Our friends are spending a lot these days.
We're trying to save money.
Our friends are spending a lot these days, but we're trying to save money.

1. My co-workers are going out to lunch.
   I'm eating a sandwich from home.
2. Our friends are driving a lot these days.
   Donna and I are taking the bus.
3. Our friends are seeing a lot of new movies.
   Donna and I are renting videos.
4. Joe is spending a lot.
   Donna is saving her money.
5. Jane is buying a new winter coat.
   Donna is using her old one.
6. Mary is using her credit card.
   Donna is paying in cash.

exercise 7

Use the verb *be* or the present continuous form of the verbs in parentheses to complete this reading. Add *too* when necessary.

Clothes, food, and cars ___are___ very expensive these days, and of course, houses ___are___ ___too___. It _________ [1] difficult to save enough money for a house, but we _________ [2] (do) everything possible to save. My wife _________ [3] (ride) the bus to work, and I _________ [4] _________ [5]. We _________ [6] (use) food coupons from the newspaper, and we _________ [7] (shop) for specials at the grocery store. We _________ [8] (try) to save every penny. There _________ [9] one big problem though. We _________ [10] (save) money, but we _________ [11] (get) very bored!

CULTURE NOTE

North Americans like to find "bargains"—things with reduced (cheaper) prices. Discounts, specials, or price reductions are common for food, restaurants, bus and airline tickets, long-distance telephone calls, cars, and other things. What things can you get at a special (cheap) price in your country?

Using What You've Learned

activity 1

Budgeting Money. Are you trying to save money? What are you doing or *not* doing? In pairs or small groups, write a list of everything you are doing and a list of everything you are not doing. Then share your ideas with the class.

example:

DOING	NOT DOING
We're making long-distance calls on Saturday.	**We're not calling long-distance on weekdays.**

activity 2

GROUP ACTIVITY

Comparing Lifestyles. What are some things you are doing these days? Are you saving money or are you spending a lot of money? Are you having fun, or are you getting bored? How about other students in your class? First, write five statements about your lifestyle—things you are or are not doing these days. Then work in a small group and compare your lifestyles.

	ACTIVITY	SAME	DIFFERENT
1.	I'm eating in restaurants.	Ali	Gloria
2.	I'm studying too much!	George	Fred
3.	______	______	______
4.	______	______	______
5.	______	______	______
6.	______	______	______
7.	______	______	______

After you have information about your classmates, make statements about them with *too, and,* and *but.*

examples: **I'm eating in restaurants, and Ali is too.**
I'm eating in restaurants, but Gloria isn't.
I'm studying too much, and George is too.

TOPIC **three**

More Prepositions of Place; There is / are + verb + -ing; It versus There

Setting the Context

prereading questions

In this picture, a TV station is filming a program. Who is in the picture, and where are these people?

BROADCASTER: "It's a busy afternoon, and we're broadcasting live from the mall. There are a lot of people shopping today! Right now, I'm standing in front of Discount Drugs. It's next to Max-Mart and across from Famous Fashions."
"Here's a shopper! Excuse me, sir. What are you buying today?"

SHOPPER: "I'm buying skis for cross-country skiing."

discussion questions

Circle T (True) or F (False).

1. T F The mall is busy today.
2. T F A television crew is broadcasting at the mall.
3. T F The announcer is standing in front of Max-Mart.
4. T F The man is buying water skis.

A. More Prepositions of Place

above / below	**next to**	**across from**
over / under	**between**	**in front of / in back of**
near / far from	**on top of**	

exercise 1 Look at this map of the mall. Imagine you are standing at the main entrance. Circle T (True) or F (False) for each sentence about the map. Correct the false sentences.

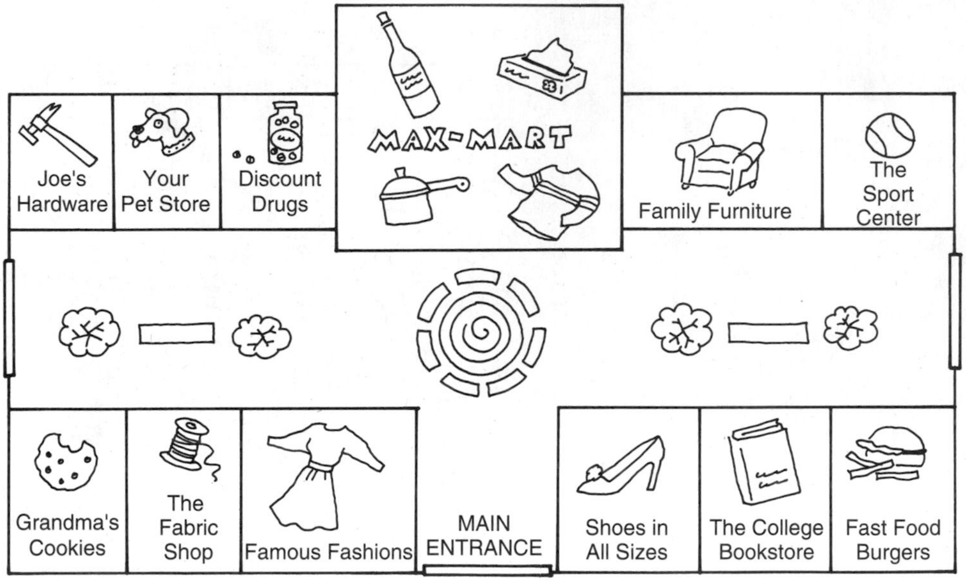

1. T (F) Discount Drugs is next to ~~Fast Food Burgers~~. Max-Mart
2. T F Discount Drugs is across from Famous Fashions.
3. F F Discount Drugs is next to Grandma's Cookies.
4. T F Grandma's Cookies is across from Joe's Hardware.
5. T F The College Bookstore is between Shoes in All Sizes and Fast Food Burgers.
6. T F Family Furniture is to the left of Max-Mart.
7. T F The Fabric Shop is between Grandma's Cookies and Famous Fashions.

8. T F The Fabric Shop is to the right of Famous Fashions.

9. T F Your Pet Store is next to Joe's Hardware.

exercise 2 Use the same map to help you. Complete these sentences with *next to, across from,* and so on.

1. There is a drugstore next to Max-Mart.
2. There is a fabric store ______________ Grandma's Cookies and Famous Fashions.
3. There is a hardware store ______________ Grandma's Cookies.
4. There is a pet store ______________ Joe's Hardware.
5. There is a drugstore ______________ Your Pet Store and Max-Mart.
6. There is a shoe store ______________ The College Bookstore.
7. There is a furniture store ______________ The College Bookstore.

B. *There is / are* with verb + *-ing*

Subject + ***be*** + **verb** + **-*ing*** **without *there***	***There*** + ***be*** + **subject** + **verb** + **-*ing*** **with *there***
A lot of people **are shopping.**	**There are** a lot of people **shopping.**
A girl **is looking** for shoes.	**There is** a girl **looking** for shoes.
A boy **is buying** some toys.	**There is** a boy **buying** some toys.

exercise 3 Use these verbs and complete the sentences. Then add two original sentences.

carrying	playing	sitting
√ listening	reading	talking

1. There are some teenage girls __listening__ to music.
2. There is a young man ______________ presents.
3. There are two young women ______________ .
4. There is a woman ______________ on a bench.
5. There is an old man ______________ the newspaper.
6. There are two little boys ______________ .

exercise 4 Use these cues (and the cues on page 59) to make sentences with *there is* or *there are* + verb + *-ing*.

examples: a parrot / say hello
There is a parrot saying hello.
two birds / sing
There are two birds singing.

1. a dog / bark
2. three cats / meow
3. a monkey / climb a ladder
4. a fish / swim in the water
5. a mouse / sit in a cage
6. two rabbits / eat lettuce

C. *It* versus *There*

	examples	notes
it	**It's** 12:30 P.M. **It's** July 4. **It's** summer. **It's** hot.	*It* is used with time and weather expressions.
there	**There are** people at the beach. **There is** a park nearby. **There are** children playing.	*There* is used to show that something exists or is in a place.

exercise 5 Tell about a year at the mall. Use *it* or *there* to complete these sentences.

1. ____It____ 's January, and ________ 's cold and snowy. ________ are a lot of people buying snow shovels.
2. ________ are a lot of people buying flowers and candy. Why? Because ________ is February, and ________ is Valentine's Day.

3. ______________ are a lot of people getting tickets to Florida. Why? Because ______________ 's March, and ______________ 's still cold and snowy in the north.

4. ______________ 's April. ______________ 's raining. ______________ are a lot of people carrying umbrellas.

5. ______________ is May. ______________ is Mother's Day. ______________ are a lot of people buying roses.

6. ______________ are a lot of people shopping for wedding presents. Why? Because ______________ 's June, and ______________ 's the month for weddings.

7. ______________ are a lot of people looking for swimming suits. Why? Because ______________ 's July, and ______________ 's hot.

8. ______________ are a lot of people buying school clothes. Why? Because ______________ is August, and ______________ 's back-to-school time.

9. ______________ 's September. ______________ 's autumn. ______________ are a lot of people buying rakes for raking leaves.

10. ______________ are a lot of people buying costumes. Why? Because ______________ is October, and ______________ is Halloween.

11. ______________ 's November. ______________ 's windy outside. ______________ are a lot of people wearing coats and gloves.

12. ______________ is December. ______________ is the holiday season. ______________ are a lot of people shopping for presents.

Most of North America has four seasons. Each season has traditional customs and special events. For each season, people may also need different clothes and equipment—shorts and swimming suits in the summer and mittens and boots in the winter, rakes in the fall and snow shovels in the winter.

Using What You've Learned

activity 1

Describing Locations. Look around your class. Who is sitting in front of you? Who is sitting next to you? Are you sitting near the door? Write two statements about your location in the classroom, but do not put your name on your paper. Your teacher will collect the papers and read them. Guess who each person is.

example: TEACHER: **I'm sitting across from Miguel. I'm sitting in front of Akiko.**

STUDENT: **It's Mei!**

activity 2

Describing Places. What is your favorite place? What is your favorite time of the year there? Is your favorite place a beach in December? Or is it a city in the spring? Imagine you are not in class, and you are at your favorite place. Describe the season and the weather, and tell about the people and things around you.

example: **It's December in Chile. It's hot. I'm sitting on the beach. There are a lot of people enjoying the beautiful weather.**

activity 3

Role-Playing Shopping Trips. In pairs or small groups, role-play the following situations.

1. You and your friend are at the bookstore. You are looking for school supplies. Ask for help.
2. You and your friend are at the hardware store. You are making bookshelves and need supplies. Ask for help.
3. You are at the drugstore. You are looking for medicine for a cold. Ask for help.

TOPIC four

Be going to; to and to the with locations; because

Setting the Context

prereading questions

In this picture, a TV news team is filming a program. Where are they filming? What are the other people in the picture doing?

A "We're standing here in front of Sam's Super Saver Gas Station. A lot of people are buying lottery tickets today because there's going to be a $20,000,000 jackpot. Excuse me, sir. Are you going to buy a lottery ticket?"

B "Yes, I am. I *know* I'm going to win. I can feel it! They're going to pick my numbers. Then I'm going to change everything in my life."

discussion questions

1. What are the people buying?
2. What is the man dreaming about?

A. *Be going to* + verb—Affirmative Statements

Subject + ***be*** + ***going to*** + **verb**

long form	contraction	notes
I **am going to study** tonight.	I'**m going to study** tonight.	*Be going to* + verb is used to talk about future plans. It is very common in conversation.
You **are going to run** tomorrow.	You'**re going to run** tomorrow.	
He / She / It } **is going to work.**	He'**s** / She'**s** / It'**s** } **going to work.**	
We / You / They } **are going to play** tennis.	We'**re** / You'**re** / They'**re** } **going to play** tennis.	

exercise 1 Underline all uses of *be going to* + verb in the opening conversation on page 62.

exercise 2 Jack is imagining that he is the lottery winner! Use these cues to make sentences about his plans.

example: buy some new clothes

Jack is going to buy some new clothes.

1. get a Rolls-Royce
2. take a long trip
3. buy presents for his family and friends
4. give money to a charity
5. build a new house
6. send his children to a good university

CULTURE NOTE

Every year Americans spend millions of dollars on lottery tickets.

B. *To* and *to the* with Locations

To or *to the* is used with some locations. With other locations, *to* or *to the* is *not* used; only the place expression is used.

to	to the	no preposition or article
I'm going to go **to church.**	I'm going to go **to the bank.**	I'm going to go **downtown.**
to church to class to school to work	to the bank to the beach to the hospital to the library to the movies to the museum to the post office to the store	downtown home (over) there

exercise 3 Make sentences with the cues below and *She's going to go.*

example: store

She's going to go to the store.

1. bank
2. post office
3. home
4. there
5. school
6. work
7. movies
8. museum
9. downtown
10. beach

C. *Be going to* + verb—Negative Statements

Subject + ***be*** + ***not*** + ***going to*** + **verb**

long form	contraction	
I **am not going to study.**	I**'m not going to study.**	
You **are not going to run.**	You**'re not going to run.**	You **aren't going to run.**
He / She / It } **is not going to eat.**	He**'s not** / She**'s not** / It**'s not** } **going to eat.**	He **isn't** / She **isn't** / It **isn't** } **going to eat.**
We / You / They } **are not going to play tennis.**	We**'re not** / You**'re not** / They**'re not** } **going to play tennis.**	We **aren't** / You **aren't** / They **aren't** } **going to play tennis.**

exercise 4 Jack is the winner of the lottery jackpot! Tell about his plans. Use *be going to* and make sentences.

example: not live in his old apartment anymore / buy a big house

Jack's not going to live in his old apartment anymore. He's going to buy a big house in the country.

1. not drive his old car anymore / buy an expensive sports car
2. not work anymore / quit his job
3. not stay home anymore / take a trip around the world
4. not do housework anymore / hire a cleaning service
5. not wear his old clothes anymore / buy designer suits
6. not use credit cards anymore / pay in cash

D. *Be going to* + verb—Questions

Statement	She's going to go shopping.
Yes/No Question	***Be* + subject + *going to* + verb**
	Is she **going to go** shopping?
Information Questions	**Question word + *be* + subject + *going to* + verb**
	What is she **going to do?** **When is** she **going to go** shopping? **Where is** she **going to go** shopping? **Why is** she **going to go** shopping?

exercise 5 Work with a partner. Ask and answer these questions.

example: A: What are you going to do after class?
B: **I'm going to go to the library.**
or **I'm going to study.**

1. Are you going to stay home tonight? What are you going to do?
2. Where are you going to be this weekend? Are you going to be at home?
3. When are you going to call your family? Are you going to call collect?
4. Are you going to go grocery shopping soon? What are you going to buy?
5. When are you going to go clothes shopping? Where are you going to go? What are you going to buy?
6. Are you going to see a movie soon? What are you going to see?

E. *Because*

Two Sentences	I'm buying a soccer ball. I'm going to play soccer.	*Because* shows the reason for something. It joins two sentences.
One Sentence	I'm buying a soccer ball **because** I'm going to play soccer.	

exercise 6 Make sentences with *because.* Use the present continuous tense and *be going to.*

example: a heavy jacket / move to Alaska

I'm looking for a heavy jacket because I'm going to move to Alaska.

1. a suitcase / take a trip
2. a nice dress / have a party
3. ice skates / take skating lessons
4. a French dictionary / study French
5. yarn / knit a sweater
6. fabric / make a skirt

exercise 7 Complete this story with the verb *be,* the present continuous tense, or *be going to* + verb. Use the verbs in parentheses. Use negative forms when you see *not.*

Jack's wife, Julie, ____is____ (be) very happy. She ____is smiling____ (smile) a lot today. Why? Because Jack ______1______ (be) the lottery winner!

Right now Julie ______2______ (not work). She ______3______ (sit) at home with her friends. She ______4______ (talk) about her travel plans. Her friends ______5______ (not listen) because they ______6______ (dream) about the lottery.

Next week Jack and Julie ______7______ (take) a long vacation. They ______8______ (travel) around the world. They ______9______ (visit) Paris, Rome, Athens, Singapore, and Tokyo. Then they ______10______ (go) to Hawaii.

Right now Jack ______11______ (shop) for things for the trip. But Jack ______12______ (not be) happy. He ______13______ (be) tired, and he ______14______ (dream) about his old life!

Using What You've Learned

activity 1

Making Plans. Imagine that *you* are the winner of the lottery jackpot! What things are you going to do and not going to do anymore? Talk about your plans in small groups. Choose one student to tell the class about your plans.

example: **Hassan is going to buy a new car, and Seiji is too. Hassan's going to buy a Jaguar, but Seiji isn't. He's going to get a Ferrari. Anne is not going to go to study English anymore. She's going to hire a translator!**

activity 2

Talking About the Future. What is your future going to bring? Are you going to take a long vacation? Are you going to find the perfect job? Are you going to meet the perfect husband or wife? Are you going to become famous? Visit your class "fortune teller" and learn about your future. In small groups, take turns being the fortune teller and the customers.

checking your progress

Check your progress with structures from Chapters One and Two. Be sure to review any problem areas.

Part 1. Choose the correct word(s) to complete each sentence.

1. Mariela _____ from Colombia
   a. am
   b. is
   c. are
2. _____ is George? He's 25.
   a. When
   b. How
   c. How old
3. Alex is doing _____ homework.
   a. his
   b. he
   c. she
4. Sandy is tired, _____ I'm not.
   a. and
   b. but
   c. because
5. Jim is going _____ .
   a. to downtown
   b. to the downtown
   c. downtown
6. Why _____ there?
   a. she is going
   b. is going she
   c. is she going
7. _____ cold outside.
   a. It's
   b. There
   c. Its
8. Al was born _____ March 18.
   a. in
   b. on
   c. at

9. _____ is Paul studying now? At the library.

a. What
b. Where
c. Why

10. Paul's house is _____ 4218 Yuma Drive.

a. in
b. on
c. at

Part 2: Circle the correct words to complete this story. Circle "X" to show that nothing is necessary.

(Its / It's)[1] almost summer vacation. We (is / are)[2] saving money now because we are (planning / planing)[3] a trip. On our vacation, we are going (to / to the)[4] beach. We are leaving (on / in)[5] Friday. We are going (X / to)[6] stay at a hotel (across from / on top of)[7] the beach. Near the hotel, (it / there)[8] is a park and a small shopping mall. It's (a / an)[9] beautiful place. My husband is excited about the trip, (and / but)[10] I am too!

CULTURE NOTE

Progress checks are very common in North American education. A common type is multiple choice. Each item has two or more choices, and you must choose the correct answer.

CHAPTER three

Friends and Family

in this chapter

The Simple Present Tense and Related Structures

Topic One: Affirmative Statements; Spelling and Pronunciation

Topic Two: Adverbs of Frequency; Questions and Short Answers; Negative Statements

Topic Three: Commands; Common Verbs + Infinitives

Topic Four: Contrast of Simple Present and Present Continuous Tenses; Nonaction Verbs: Object Pronouns

TOPIC **one**

Affirmative Statements; Spelling and Pronunciation

Setting the Context

prereading questions Which picture shows the typical American family? Which picture looks like your family?

The North American Family

We have many different kinds of families in North America. There are large families, like the Sommas. They have eight children. Loretta and Steve Mason have a small family. They have two children. Some children live in single-parent homes, like Ricky Jones. He lives with his mother, Rita. In today's families, the parents and the children help around the house. Everyone does different chores like vacuuming, washing clothes, and taking out the garbage.

discussion questions

Circle T (True) or F (False).

1. T F Mr. and Mrs. Somma have a small family.
2. T F Loretta and Steve Mason have eight children.
3. T F Rita Jones has one child.
4. T F Ricky Jones lives in a single-parent home.
5. T F In today's families, only the parents work around the house.

A. The Verb *Have*—Affirmative Statements

Subject + *have*	**Subject + *has***
I / You / We / They **have** a problem.	He / She / It **has** a problem.

exercise 1 Use *have* or *has* to complete these sentences.

1. I'm Rose Somma. There are ten people in my family! I _have_ a mother, a father, and seven sisters and brothers. I also _____ many cousins. My oldest cousin is married. She _____ a daughter and a baby boy. My other cousins aren't married.

2. I'm Steve Mason. Loretta and I _____ a small family. I come from a bigger family. I _____ three sisters and two brothers. All of us are married. We all _____ children too. So my mother _____ eleven grandchildren.

3. I'm Ricky Jones. We _____ a very small family. I _____ only a mother. But my mother _____ five brothers and sisters, so we _____ a lot of relatives.

CULTURE NOTE

In about 50 percent of U.S. families, both the husband and the wife work. Is this the same or different in your country?

B. The Verb *Do*—Affirmative Statements

Subject + *do*	**Subject + *does***
I / You / We / They **do** a lot of work.	He / She / It **does** a lot of work.

expressions

	do* + verb + *-ing
do dishes	**do** cleaning
do errands	**do** gardening
do homework	**do** (grocery) shopping
do housework	
do laundry	

***exercise* 2** Use *do* or *does* to complete this reading.

We have a lot of housework in the Somma family. We all __do__ chores in our house. My mother _____ (1) the grocery shopping. She also _____ (2) the laundry, but my older sisters _____ (3) the ironing. My younger sisters _____ (4) the vacuuming. I _____ (5) the dishes every morning, and my brother _____ (6) the dishes every night. My father _____ (7) most of the cooking. He also _____ (8) the yard work. We all _____ (9) housework every day. We try hard to keep our house clean!

In North America, the entire family often helps with housework. Even young children have household chores. Women still do most of the housework, but today, husbands help much more than in the past.

C. Simple Present Tense of Other Verbs—Affirmative Statements

Subject + verb	Subject + verb + *-s*	notes
I / You / We / They } **work** a lot.	He / She / It } **works** a lot.	The simple present tense is used to talk about facts, opinions, and habits or schedules. Time expressions with this tense include *every day, every week, always,* and *sometimes.*

***exercise* 3** Use *work* or *works* to complete this reading.

Joe Somma is nineteen years old. He ___works___ at the grocery store. He ___________ (2) forty hours a week. His younger brothers ___________ (2) at the car wash. They ___________ (3) part-time, twenty hours a week. Joe's father ___________ (4) at the gas station, and his mother ___________ (5) at the department store. The whole family ___________ (6) very hard.

Culture Note

Many American and Canadian young people have jobs while they are going to school. At age 16, Americans can work legally, so many high school students work after school and on weekends. University students frequently have jobs to help pay for their education.

D. Pronunciation

/s/ after /f/, /k/, /p/, and /t/		/z/ after /b/, /d/, /l/, /m/, /n/, /r/, /v/, and vowel sounds		
laughs*	sleeps	robs	comes	loves
works	hates	needs	listens	plays
		calls	tours	sees

*In this case, the pronunciation of *gh* is /f/.

exercise 4 Look at the list of verbs above. Repeat the words after your teacher. Underline the letters for each sound before the letter *s*.

example: lau gh s

wor ks

exercise 5 Use these cues to make sentences about Rose. Then work with a partner and take turns reading the sentences aloud. Pay attention to the pronunciation of the *-s* ending.

example: get up very early

Rose gets up very early.

1. eat breakfast
2. drink a cup of tea
3. walk to school
4. work hard at school
5. think a lot about the future
6. want a job at a newspaper

exercise 6 Use these cues to make sentences about Mrs. Somma. Work with a partner, and take turns reading the sentences aloud. Pay attention to the pronunciation of the *-s* ending.

example: listen to the radio every morning.

Mrs. Somma listens to the radio every morning.

1. prepare breakfast
2. drive to the train station
3. arrive at work at 10:00 A.M.
4. come home at 6:00 P.M.
5. clean the house at night
6. stay up late

E. Spelling and Pronunciation (1)

words ending in consonant + *y*		words ending in vowel + *y*		notes
cry	cri**es**	buy	buy**s**	Verbs with *y* endings sometimes change spelling. These verbs have the /z/ pronunciation.
study	studi**es**	enjoy	enjoy**s**	
try	tri**es**	play	play**s**	
		say	say**s**	

exercise 7

Use the verbs in parentheses to complete the readings about the Somma family. Pay attention to pronunciation and spelling.

1. My brother Mike ___tries___ (try) hard in school. He ______(1) (study) a lot. He also ______(2) (spend) a lot of time on sports. He ______(3) (play) a lot of different sports. He especially ______(4) (enjoy) swimming and soccer. He ______(5) (hate) to be bored.

2. My father ______(1) (work) very hard. In fact, he usually ______(2) (stay) at the gas station until late at night. He ______(3) (say) that he ______(4) (try) to take a vacation. But he never ______(5) (have) time. He ______(6) (worry) a lot about money. I worry a lot about him. Money ______(7) (buy) food, but money doesn't buy good health.

F. Spelling and Pronunciation (2)

words ending in *ch, sh, ss, x,* and *z*				notes
watch	watch**es**	fix	fix**es**	Add *-es* to words ending in *ch, sh, ss, x,* and *z.* The pronunciation is /ez/ or /iz/.
wash	wash**es**	buzz	buzz**es**	
kiss	kiss**es**			

words ending in *o*				
do	do**es**	potato	potato**es**	Words ending in *o* sometimes add *-es* . The pronunciation is /z/.
go	go**es**	tomato	tomato**es**	

exercise 8 Complete this reading with the verbs in parentheses. Pay attention to pronunciation and spelling.

My mother ___does___ (do) many things for me. Early in the morning, she _____1_____ (push) me out of bed. She _____2_____ (fix) breakfast and then _____3_____ (wash) the dishes. She _____4_____ (kiss) me good-bye and _____5_____ (watch) me walk down the block to school. Then she quickly _____6_____ (do) some housework before she _____7_____ (go) to work. My mom never _____8_____ (relax).

exercise 9 Complete this reading with the simple present forms of the verbs in parentheses. Pay attention to spelling.

Ricky Jones ___enjoys___ (enjoy) family picnics. His mother _____1_____ (have) a large family, and they _____2_____ (get) together for picnics in the summer. Rita Jones _____3_____ (fix) salad and dessert, and her brothers and sisters _____4_____ (buy) food for a barbecue. Grandma always _____5_____ (make) cookies.

Ricky _____6_____ (play) ball with his older cousins. He _____7_____ (try) hard to hit the ball, and sometimes he _____8_____ (do). He _____9_____ (watch) his cousins hit home runs all the time. He _____10_____ (enjoy) the games, but his grandma _____11_____ (kiss) him too much!

Using What You've Learned

activity 1

Telling About Families. Do you have a small family or a large family? Write a paragraph about your family. Use the ideas in exercise 1 to help you. Then work with a partner. Read your paragraph to your partner. Your partner is going to write down your paragraph. Finally, listen to your partner's paragraph and write it down.

activity 2

Talking About Housework. What are the chores in a typical house? Who does the chores? In a small group, take turns telling about the Sommas and their chores. (See exercise 2.) Then fill in the chart about your family. Write in the names of your family members on the chart. Put checks (√) in the boxes. Tell the students in your group who does chores in your home.

The Somma Family

	Rose	Mother	Father	Sisters	Brothers
the cleaning	√	√	√	√	√
the cooking			√		
the dishes	√			√	√
the grocery shopping		√			
the laundry		√		√	
the yard work			√		

Your Family

the cleaning					
the cooking					
the dishes					
the grocery shopping					
the laundry					
the yard work					

activity 3 **Telling Stories.** Read the paragraph in exercise 3 again about Joe's work. Write a different paragraph about Joe and his family. Give Joe and his family new lives. Change their jobs and schedules. Then work in small groups and read your new paragraphs to each other.

activity 4 **Talking About Relatives.** Bring a picture of one person in your family. Write a short paragraph about your relative. *Don't write his or her name.* Your teacher will collect your paragraphs and pictures and put them around the room. Look at the pictures and read the other students' paragraphs. Can you find the relative of each person in the class?

activity 5 **Talking About Family Holidays.** Does your family have a special time or a special holiday together? In small groups, tell about it. When is the holiday or special day? Who comes? What do you do? What do you eat?

GROUP ACTIVITY

TOPIC two

Adverbs of Frequency; Questions and Short Answers; Negative Statements

Setting the Context

prereading questions

Who lives here? Is his room neat?

Life Is Tough

Mothers! They can drive you crazy! How often does your mom tell you to clean up your room? My mother always tells me to pick up my clothes, put away my books, make my bed, etc., etc., etc. I really try to make my room neat, but I usually forget. Then she gets upset. Sure, it's true. My mom doesn't have time to do everything. But I don't either.

discussion questions

Circle T (True) or F (False).

1. T F Ricky's mother doesn't drive him crazy.
2. T F His mother never tells him to clean up his room.
3. T F He always remembers to make his room neat.
4. T F His mother has a lot of time.

A. Adverbs of Frequency—*always, usually, often, sometimes, seldom, rarely, never*

Subject + adverb + verb

100%	**always**	I	**always**	get up	early.
90%	**usually/generally**	You			
75%	**often**	We			
50%	**sometimes**	They			
10%	**seldom/rarely**	Bill	**never**	gets up	early.
0%	**never**	Sam			
		Mary			

exercise 1

Tell about your *own* habits and activities. Use the cues at the top of page 81. Use one of these adverbs in each sentence: *always, usually, often, sometimes, seldom, rarely, never.*

example: go to bed late

I sometimes go to bed late.
or **I always go to bed late.**
or **I never go to bed late.**

1. get up early
2. eat a big breakfast
3. take the bus to school
4. drive to school
5. get to class on time
6. have lunch
7. read the local newspaper
8. cook dinner
9. do my homework
10. study English grammar very carefully

B. Adverbs of Frequency with the Verb *be*

Subject + *be* + adverb of frequency

				notes
I	am	**always**	hungry.	With the verb *be,* the adverbs of frequency come after the subject + verb.
She	is	**often**	late.	
We	are	**usually**	tired.	

exercise 2 Tell about your roommate, husband, wife, or friend. Use an adverb of frequency in each sentence. Use the cues below.

example: be late

My husband is always late.

1. be kind
2. be happy
3. be nervous
4. be bored
5. be lonely
6. be busy

C. Questions with *who*

questions	short answers with *do* or *does*	
Who+ verb+ -s(+ object)	***Affirmative***	***Negative***
Who cleans the house?	I / You / We / They } **do.**	I / You / We / They } **don't.**
Who washes the dishes?	He / She / It } **does.**	He / She / It } **doesn't.**

Note: Questions with *who* are usually singular.

exercise 3 Look back at your chore chart from Activity 2 on page 78. Work with a partner. Use those cues to ask and answer questions. Make questions with *who.* Give short answers with *do* or *does.* Then add questions from the pie chart below.

example: usually wash the dishes

A: **In your family, who usually fixes breakfast?**
B: **My mother does.**
or **My father does.**
or **I do. My wife never does.**

D. Negative Statements

Long Form

Subject + *do not* + verb	Subject + *does not* + verb
I / You / We / They **do not wash** dishes.	He / She / It **does not wash** dishes.

Contraction

Subject + *don't* + verb	Subject + *doesn't* + verb
I / You / We / They **don't cook.**	He / She / It **doesn't cook.**

exercise 4 Use *don't* or *doesn't* to complete these sentences. Then decide if the statements are true. Write *true* or *false* after each statement.

1. People ___don't___ like to clean the bathroom. ___true___
2. Most people ___don't___ meow. __________

3. A cat __________ bark. __________

4. I __________ teach English. __________

5. This book __________ have 10,000 pages. __________

6. A house __________ have doors. __________

7. People __________ have four legs. __________

8. I __________ speak Chinese. __________

exercise 5 Write five things you *don't* ever do. Write five things your friend, roommate, husband, or wife *doesn't* ever do. Then work in groups and share your information.

example: **I don't smoke. I don't drive fast.**
My roommate doesn't go to bed early. She doesn't speak my language.

ME	AND MY __________
1. __________	__________
2. __________	__________
3. __________	__________
4. __________	__________
5. __________	__________

E. *Yes/no* Questions

***Do* + subject + verb**

Do { I / you / we / they } **clean** everyday?

***Does* + subject + verb**

Does { he / she / it } **help** very often?

exercise 6 Work with a partner. Ask and answer the questions on page 84. Listen when your partner asks a question. *Don't read the question. Look at each other!*

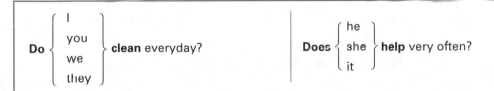

STUDENT A

1. Do you have a small family or a large family?
2. Does your family live in this city?
3. Do you often call your friends in your country?
4. Do your relatives all live in your country?
5. Now ask two more questions with *do* or *does.*

STUDENT B

1. In your country, do fathers kiss sons?
2. Does your mother write to you?
3. Do your brothers or sisters speak English?
4. Do your friends call you long-distance?
5. Now ask two more questions with *do* or *does.*

F. Information Questions with *how often*

Statement	I study every night. She studies every night.
Yes/No Question	***Do*** **or** ***does*** **+ subject + verb** **Do** you **study** every night? **Does** she **study every night?**
Information Question	**Question word +** ***do*** **or** ***does*** **+ subject + verb** **How often do** you **study?** **How often does** she **study?**

exercise 7 Work with a partner. Ask and answer questions about the people on page 85. Make questions with *how often.*

example: A: **How often does she study?**
B: **She studies every night.**

1.

Clean the apartment?
Every week!

2.

Put toys away?
Every night!

3.

Make dinner?
Once or twice a week!

4.

Wash the dishes?
Every day!

5.

Do the watering?
Once a week.

6.

Make long-distance calls?
Four or five times a day.

Using What You've Learned

activity 1

Asking Questions. Write eight interesting questions with *how often.* Then work with a partner. Take turns asking and answering each other's questions.

1. How often do you call home?
2. How often ____________________
3. How often ____________________
4. How often ____________________
5. How often ____________________
6. How often ____________________
7. How often ____________________

activity 2

Asking Americans Questions. A questionnaire is a list of questions. Write a questionnaire with eight questions about American family life. Write questions about things you really want to learn about. Then ask three or more Americans these questions. Finally, share the answers with the class.

example: **Do you work?**
Who cooks in your house?
How often do you shop for groceries?
Does your husband wash the clothes?

TOPIC **three**

Commands: Common Verbs + Infinitives

Setting the Context

prereading questions

Where does this boy do his homework?

Where do you do your homework?

Parents and Children

LORETTA: Michael, you have to move your books. We need to set the table for dinner.

MICHAEL: I don't want to set the table now. I'm still doing my homework.

LORETTA: But you need to help around the house sometimes! You know that.

MICHAEL: I know, but I have to finish my math homework first.

LORETTA: OK. Turn off the TV, and let's do the homework together. Then after we finish, let's set the table. OK?

discussion questions

Circle T (True) or F (False).

1. T F It's time for lunch at the Mason house.

2. T F Michael needs to set the table.

3. T F Michael has spelling homework.

4. T F Loretta wants to do the homework with Michael.

A. Commands

affirmative	negative	notes
Sit down, please.	**Don't stand** up.	Use this form for *you*. For politeness, add *please*.
Let's sit down.	**Let's not stand** up.	Use this form for *we*.

exercise 1 Underline all commands in the opening conversation on page 86.

exercise 2 Loretta is talking to Michael. Use these verbs to make commands. Use *don't* for negative commands.

be	comb	fight	√ take	watch
clean	do	√ make	wash	

1. ___Take___ out the garbage.
2. ___Don't make___ a mess! (negative)
3. ________________ your room!
4. ________________ your face!
5. ________________ your hair!
6. ________________ your homework!
7. ________________ with your brother! (negative)
8. ________________ late! (negative)
9. ________________ TV until you finish your homework! (negative)
10. ________________ the dishes!

exercise 3 Now Loretta and Michael will work together. Change Loretta's commands from the *you* form to the *we* form.

example: Wash the dishes!
Let's wash the dishes.

1. Clean your room!
2. Make your bed!
3. Take out the garbage!
4. Do the laundry!
5. Read your assignment!
6. Practice your grammar exercises!

CULTURE NOTE

North Americans often use *Let's* . . . (Let's go. Let's finish the work.) because it's more polite than a command (Go! Finish the work!). You can make any command more polite by saying *please*. (Please sit down. Give me that book, please.)

B. Verbs with Infinitives

verbs	examples	notes
hate	I **hate to clean** the house.	The infinitive is *to* + simple verb. Some sentences follow this pattern: Subject + verb 1 + infinitive (*to* + verb 2). The first verb can be in any tense. The second verb is always the simple form.
have	We **have to clean** the house today.	
know how	I **know how to do** laundry, but I **don't know how to iron**.	
like	I **like to read**.	
love	I **love to listen** to music.	
need	We **need to do** the laundry.	
plan	I **plan to study** tonight.	
want	We **want to relax** this weekend.	

exercise 4 Use *want to* to make complete sentences about the children on page 89.

example: become a doctor

help sick people

She wants to become a doctor.

She wants to help sick people.

I want to help sick people.

1. live in Paris
be an artist

2. work very hard
build bridges

3. open a restaurant
become famous chefs

4. be very rich
have lots and lots of money

5. be police officers
stop drug dealers

exercise 5 Work with a partner. Ask and answer questions with the following cues and *know how to*. Then add six questions of your own.

example: make Arabic food

A: **Do you know how to make Arabic food?**

B: **Yes, I do. I like to eat Arabic food a lot.**

or **No, I don't. I don't know how to cook!**

1. make Chinese food
2. bake a cake
3. iron
4. play Monopoly
5. dance
6. use a computer

7. ______________________ **10.** ______________________

8. ______________________ **11.** ______________________

9. ______________________ **12.** ______________________

exercise 6

Use these verbs to complete the following conversations. Use an infinitive in each sentence.

1. do help study √wash

RITA: Ricky, you have ___to wash___ the dishes tonight.

RICKY: I don't want ______________ the dishes, Mom. Besides, I need ______________ my lesson.

RITA: You need ______________ around the house too!

2. do clean cut relax

STEVEN: I don't like ______________ housework.

LORETTA: Well, I hate ______________ the grass, but I cut it. Come on. We need ______________ the windows.

STEVEN: OK. But then I want ______________ all day.

exercise 7

Complete this conversation. Use the simple or the infinitive form of the verbs in parentheses.

HUSBAND: Let's ___go___ (go) to a movie tonight. I want ______________ (1) (see) *Superman VI.*

WIFE: Well, we need ______________ (2) (find) a baby-sitter first.

HUSBAND: ______________ (3) (call) my mother. She usually likes ______________ (4) (baby-sit) for her grandson. Alex likes ______________ (5) (play) at Grandma's house.

WIFE: OK, but somebody needs ______________ (6) (do) the laundry first.

HUSBAND: ______________ (7) (do) the laundry, and then let's ______________ (8) (go) to the movie.

WIFE: Fine, but you have ______________ (help) me.
9

HUSBAND: Well, I don't really want ______________ (do) laundry.
10

WIFE: And I don't want ______________ (see) *Superman VI.* Let's ______________ (stay) home. Let's ______________ (rent) videos.
11 / 13 / 12

HUSBAND: Great idea! *Superman I, II, III, IV,* and *V!*

Using What You've Learned

activity 1

Telling People to Do Things. Look at the pictures. Give a command for each picture.

activity 2

GROUP ACTIVITY

Making Suggestions. Is it easy to learn English? Is it fun? Do you have some good ideas about learning English? In small groups, take turns making suggestions. Use *let's.* Then as a class, compare all the suggestions. Who has the best ideas?

examples: **Let's invite some North American students to our class.**

Let's meet outside of class to practice!

activity 3

Talking About Likes, Needs, and Wants. In groups, take turns asking one another these questions.

1. Name two things you like to do. Name two things you don't like to do.
2. What are two things you need to do today? What are two things you have to do this week?
3. What do you want to do this evening? What do you plan to do this weekend?

TOPIC four

Contrast of Simple Present and Present Continuous Tenses; Nonaction Verbs; Object Pronouns

Setting the Context

prereading questions

Describe each picture. What relationship do these people have?

Best Friends

Your best friend is your very special friend. Your best friend knows you well and understands you. You help each other, and you listen to each other. You tell each other the truth. You laugh together, and you cry together. You remember the good times, and you forget the bad times. You sometimes have fights, but you always love each other.

discussion questions

Circle T (True) or F (False).

1. T F Your best friend rarely understands you.
2. T F Friends tell each other the truth.
3. T F Friends never cry.
4. T F You never fight with a friend.

A. Simple Present Tense Versus Present Continuous Tense

	examples	notes
Simple Present Tense	I always **tell** my friends everything.	The simple present tense is used for facts, opinions, or repeated actions. (See page 74.)
Present Continuous Tense	Right now he's **telling** a story to his friend.	The present continuous tense is used for actions that are happening now. (See page 39.)

exercise 1 **Information Gap.** Here are two charts with different information. Ask a partner questions to complete your chart.

example: B: **What is Sally doing now?**

A: **What does John do every Monday morning?**

student a

	Now	*Every Monday Morning*	*Every Saturday Night*
Sally	sleep	__________	__________
Sam	__________	work at McDonald's	__________
John	eat a snack	__________	__________
Jane	__________	work in a hospital	visit family

student b

	Now	*Every Monday Morning*	*Every Saturday Night*
Sally	________________	baby-sit	work at a movie theater
Sam	read a magazine	____________________	go out with friends
John	________________	play tennis	stay home
Jane	take a nap	____________________	________________

exercise 2 Complete these sentences. Use the simple present or the present continuous tense.

1. Right now my mother (or sister, brother, etc.) ________________.
2. On Friday nights, I ________________.
3. Our teacher always ________________.
4. My best friend often ________________.
5. At this moment, my friend ________________.
6. My friend and I never ________________.

B. Nonaction Verbs

Feelings, Opinions, and Thoughts

	examples	**notes**
be **forget** **hate** **like** **love** **mean** **need** **remember** **understand** **want**	I **am** his friend. I **forget** his name. They **hate** to be late. He **likes** to get together with old friends. They **love** their dog. What **does** it **mean?** I **need** friends. I **don't remember.** I **don't understand** that word. I **want** to know.	These verbs describe feelings and thoughts. They also describe things we own or possess. Because the verbs do not describe actions, they are used in the simple tenses (simple present, simple past, etc.). They are not generally used in the continuous tenses, even when the time is *now.*

Possession

	examples	notes
belong to **have** **own**	It **doesn't belong to** me. I **have** two close friends. I **own** an old car.	(See page 96 for more information on *have.*)

exercise 3 Work with a partner. Take turns asking and answering these questions.

1. Do you remember the first day of class?
2. Do you like American food?
3. Do you understand the news on TV?
4. Do you need to spend time alone?
5. Do you own a car?
6. Does this book belong to you?

exercise 4 Complete these questions. Then work with a partner. Take turns asking and answering each other's questions.

1. Do you remember ______________________________?
2. Do you like ______________________________?
3. Do you understand ______________________________?
4. Do you need ______________________________?
5. Do you own ______________________________?

C. *Have* — Simple Present Versus Present Continuous Tense

Possession

	examples	notes
have	I **have** a new car. She **has** a headache.	Use the simple present tense.

Other Expressions

	examples	notes
have a problem	I'**m having** a problem with my boyfriend.	Use the present continuous tense for actions happening *now.*
have a good time	They'**re having** a good time at the party.	
have a party	She'**s having** a party at her apartment.	
have breakfast (lunch, dinner, etc.)	We'**re having** a snack because we're hungry.	

exercise 5 Complete these sentences with *have/has* or *am/is/are having.*

1. I ___have___ a car. I ___am having___ problems with my car.
2. I ______________ a party right now. Come on over.
3. I ______________ a headache. I'm sorry, but I can't come.
4. I ______________ no friends here.
5. I ______________ a problem with this question.
6. My friend ______________ a close friend—me!
7. Who ______________ my grammar book?

D. Pronouns and Possessive Adjectives

subject pronouns		possessive adjectives		object pronouns	
singular	**plural**	**singular**	**plural**	**singular**	**plural**
I	we	my	our	me	us
you	you	your	your	you	you
he	they	his	their	him	them
she		her		her	
it		its		it	

Object Pronouns

Subject + verb + object (object pronoun)

I	love	my mother.	=	I	love	her.
He	loves	English.	=	He	loves	it.
He	loves	his teachers.	=	He	loves	them.

exercise 6 Change the words in parentheses to object pronouns.

1. I often write to (my girlfriend) ____her____.
2. My mother is old. I always help (my mother) ______________.
3. My cousin and his wife live in Vancouver. I often visit (my cousin and his wife) ______________.
4. We are a nice class. Don't forget (all the people in this class) ______________.
5. My grandfather lives in a small village. I often think about (my grandfather) ______________.
6. Where is my grammar book? Oh, no! I lost (my grammar book) ______________!
7. It's our grammar teacher's birthday. I have a present for (our grammar teacher) ______________.
8. Every Sunday my parents call. Every Wednesday I call (my parents) ______________.
9. My friends are in my country. I miss (my friends) ______________.

exercise 7 Use the simple present tense to complete this reading.

MY BEST FRIEND

I _____have_____ (have) a best friend. My best friend _____ (be)
1

a very special person, and I _____ (love) her very much. We
2

_____ (have/always) fun together. She _____ (know) me,
3 4

and she _____ (understand) me very well.
5

Now my friend _____ (live) far away. It _____ (mean)
6 7

we _____ (not see) each other very often. We _____ (have)
8 9

to write letters. I _____ (like) to read her letters because she
10

_____ (tell/always) interesting stories.
11

I _____ (feel/sometimes) lonely because she _____ (be)
12 13

far away. I _____ (miss) her very much. But today I _____
14 15

(feel) very happy because she is going to come for a visit. I _____ (be)
16

excited.

exercise 8 Circle the correct pronouns in these readings.

1. Hi! (I / My / Me) am Chris Hill. My best friend is my dog, Honey.

(She / Her) is a good dog. I love (she / her). She follows (I / my / me)
1 2 3

everywhere. I'm never lonely. Every day my friends come over, and

(she / her) plays with (they / their / them). Someday she will have puppies.
4 5

My friends each want one of (she / her) puppies.

2. My best friend is (I / my / me)$_1$ computer, Mac. I spend six to ten hours a day with (it / its)$_2$. A computer is really a great friend. I always tell (it / its)$_3$ what to do. Sometimes it doesn't understand (I / my / me)$_4$. Then (we / our / us)$_5$ spend hours together. We try to communicate. We try to solve (we / our / us)$_6$ problems. In the end, (we / our / us)$_7$ always find an answer. I appreciate Mac.

George Lynch, 28, Computer consultant, My computer.

3. My best friend is my husband. He always understands (I / my / me)$_1$ problems. He always asks (I / my / me)$_2$ for opinions. He respects (I / my / me)$_3$. People are always happy to see (we / our / us)$_4$ together. After forty years of marriage, (he / his / him)$_5$ is still my best friend, and I still love (he / his / him)$_6$.

Using What You've Learned

activity

Writing About Friends. Write a short paragraph about a friend. Why is your friend special? What do you do together? Where is your friend now? What is he or she doing?

CHAPTER four

Health Care

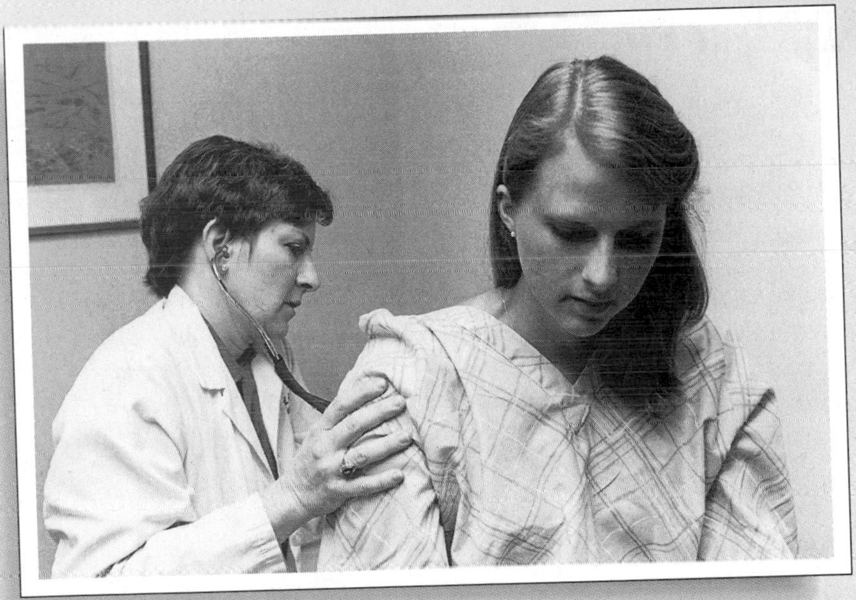

in this chapter

Modal Auxiliaries and Related Structures

Topic One:	*Can* and *can't;* Yes/No Questions; Questions with *when, where,* and *how*
Topic Two:	*Could* and *would* with Requests and Desires
Topic Three:	*Should, must,* and *have to*
Topic Four:	*Might* with Possibilities; Simple Future Tense with *will; or*

TOPIC one

Can and Can't; Questions with When, Where, and How

Setting the Context

prereading questions

Look at the picture of a father and son on page 103. How old is the father? How old does he look?

Physical Fitness

SEYMOUR: When are you going to start taking care of yourself, Dad?
DAD: I can't. I'm too old.
SEYMOUR: You can! It's never too late. You can change your eating habits and start exercising.
DAD: Where can I exercise? I can't go to the gym. I'm too embarrassed. I look too fat.
SEYMOUR: How can you say that, Dad? There are a lot of heavy or overweight people at the gym. They're trying to get into shape.
DAD: I can't go there. I really can't.
SEYMOUR: Well, then you can walk outside or in the mall.
DAD: Son, I can't reach the TV. Please change the channel and pass me another bag of potato chips.

discussion questions

1. Why does Seymour worry about his father?
2. Does Seymour's father want to go to the gym? Why or why not?
3. Do you think Seymour's father will start exercising?

A. Modal Auxiliaries

The modal auxiliaries are *can, could, may, might, must, ought to, shall, should, will,* and *would.* These are special verb forms in English. They do not change forms; they do not add *-s* or *-ed.* They change meaning. Each word has several different meanings.

Expressing Present Abilities—*can* and *can't (cannot)*

affirmative	negative	notes
Subject + *can* + verb	**Subject + *can't (cannot)* + verb**	
I / You / He / She / It / We / They **can run** fast.	I / You / He / She / It / We / They **can't swim.** / **cannot swim.**	*Can* and *can't (cannot)* are used to tell about abilities. The simple form of a verb always follows *can, can't,* and other modal auxiliaries.

exercise 1 Underline all uses of *can* and *can't* in the conversation on page 102.

exercise 2 Some people like to play sports for physical fitness. Which sports do you play? Make sentences with *can* or *can't*.

example: swim
I can swim.
or **I can't swim.**

1. run a mile
2. do aerobics
3. play soccer
4. ski
5. dive
6. play tennis
7. lift weights
8. skate

B. Yes/No Questions and Short Answers

yes/no questions	possible answers: Affirmative	possible answers: Negative
Can + subject + *verb*	Subject + *can*	Subject + *can't*
Can {I / you / he / she / it / we / they} **swim** here?	Yes, {I / you / he / she / it / we / they} **can.**	No, {I / you / he / she / it / we / they} **can't.**

exercise 3 Work with a partner. Use *can* to make questions about these actions. Take turns asking and answering the questions.

example: walk ten miles
A: **Can you walk ten miles?**
B: **Yes, I can.**
or **No, I can't.**

1. touch your toes
2. lift fifty pounds
3. run a mile
4. change a flat tire
5. cook Chinese food
6. dance the tango
7. play the piano
8. read Italian
9. sing well
10. ride a bicycle ten miles
11. do six push-ups
12. do three chin-ups
13. ski
14. speak Russian
15. use a computer
16. whistle
17. ____________________
18. ____________________

exercise 4 In negative statements, people often use *don't* or *doesn't know how to* instead of *can't* or *cannot.* Make sentences with *can* and *not know how to* about the following people.

example: **He can swim, but he doesn't know how to water-ski.**

1.

2.

3.

4.

5.

C. Questions with *When* and *Where*

information questions					possible answers
Question + *can* + subject + *verb*					
When	**can**	we	**swim**	here?	After 4:30.
Where	**can**	he	**buy**	a bicycle?	At City Sports Store.

D. Questions with *How*

information questions	possible answers	notes
How **+ adverb +** ***can*** **+ subject + verb**		
How far / **How fast** / **How long** } **can** you **run?**	I can run three miles. I can't run very fast! I can't run for very long at all. I can run for about fifteen minutes.	*How far . . .* ? asks about distance. *How fast . . .* ? asks about speed. *How long . . .* ? asks about length or period of time. *For* + period of time is often used in answers.

exercise 5 Work in pairs. Write questions for the answers. Then take turns asking and answering.

example: A: How far can you run? (run)
B: **I can run five miles easily!**

1. ______________________ (run)

Not far at all!

2. ______________________ (ride your bicycle)

Not very fast at all!

3. ______________________ (ski)

Too fast!

4. ______________________ (hold 100 pounds)

Not long at all!

5. ______________________ (throw a football)

Really far!

6. ______________________ (swim)

Not very far!

Using What You've Learned

activity 1

Information Gap. Work with a partner. Use question words and *can I* to make questions using these cues. Then take turns asking and answering the questions. Student A should cover up student B's answers. Student B should cover up Student A's questions.

example: where / play tennis for free — at the high school

A: **Where can I play tennis for free?**

B: **You can play tennis at the high school.**

STUDENT A	STUDENT B
1. where / buy running shoes	at any shoe store
2. where / play basketball	at the high school
3. when / use the swimming pool	from 7:00 A.M. to 7.00 P.M.
4. where / rent a bicycle	at a bike shop
5. when / go to aerobics class	at 6:00 P.M.

activity 2

Giving and Getting Information. Think of six interesting questions to ask other students. Write three questions with *where can I . . .* ? and three with *when can I . . .* ? Then ask six people your questions.

examples: **Where can I find good Japanese food?**
When can I have lunch with you?

activity 3

Talking About Activities. What sports can you do? What languages can you speak, read, or write? Work in a small group. Take turns asking and answering questions with *can.* Use the following ideas, and add categories and activities of your own.

GAMES	HOBBIES	SPORTS	
play checkers	cook	bowl	____________
play chess	knit	play golf, soccer, etc.	____________
____________	make furniture	skate	____________
____________	play a musical instrument	____________	____________
	____________	____________	
	____________		

TOPIC two

Could and *would* with Requests and Desires

Setting the Context

prereading questions

Look at this picture. What problem does the man have? Who is he calling for help?

A Day at the Dentist's

RECEPTIONIST: Good afternoon. Could you hold please? [*click*] Thank you for holding. Can I help you?

ALEX: Yes, thank you. I would like to make a dental appointment.

RECEPTIONIST: Is this for a checkup?

ALEX: No, it's an emergency! I would like to see the dentist today. I have a bad toothache.

RECEPTIONIST: Is 4:30 OK?

ALEX: Could I come at 5:00? I have to work until 4:30.

RECEPTIONIST: The last appointment is 4:45. Can you come then?

ALEX: Yes. I need help! See you at 4:45, and thanks!

discussion questions

1. Why does Alex need to see the dentist?
2. Can he see the dentist at five o'clock?
3. What time is his appointment?

A. Making Requests for Permission

questions	possible answers		notes
***Could* + *I* or *we* + verb**	***Affirmative***	***Negative***	
Could I make a five o'clock appointment?	Yes, of course.	No, our last appointment is at 4:45.	In these cases, we want to do something and are asking for someone's help or permission.
Could we talk to Dr. Smith?	Sure. (informal)	Sorry, but she isn't here.	

exercise 1 Use *could I* to make requests.

example: see the doctor
Could I see the doctor, please?

1. make a dental appointment

2. make an appointment with a doctor

3. talk with a nurse

4. have some aspirin

5. get a prescription

6. talk to a pharmacist

B. Making Requests for Action

questions	possible answers: Affirmative	possible answers: Negative	notes
Could + {you / he / she / it / they} + verb			
Could you help me, please?	Certainly.	Sorry, but I can't.	In these cases, we are asking someone else to do something.
Could they help me?	No problem! (informal)	Sorry, it's not possible.	

exercise 2 Use *could you* to make requests.

example: find a Band-Aid
Could you find a Band-Aid, please?

1. help me
2. give me some information
3. fill this prescription for me
4. explain these instructions
5. tell me the meaning of this word

C. Expressing Desires and Making Requests

statements with nouns	statements with infinitives	notes
Subject + *would like* + noun	**Subject + *would like* + infinitive**	
I **would like** some aspirin.	We **would like to buy** some aspirin, please.	*Would like* is used to tell our desires and to make requests. It is more polite than *want to.*
I**'d** also **like** some cold medicine.	We**'d** also **like to get** medicine.	The contracted form of *would* is *'d.*

exercise 3 Use the pictures to make statements with *would like to.*

example: buy

I would like to buy some aspirin, please.

1.

buy

2.

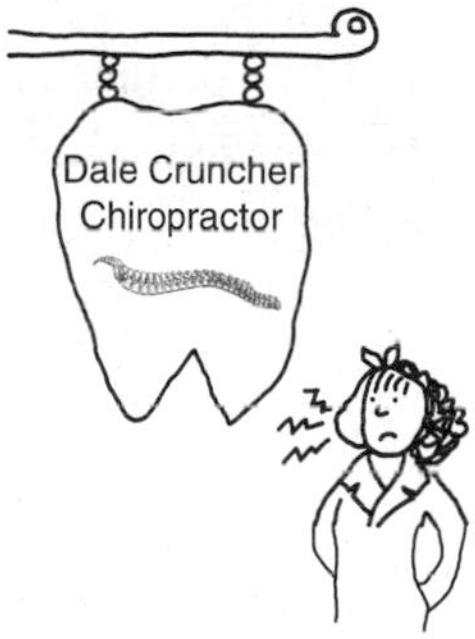

make an appointment with

3.

talk to

4.

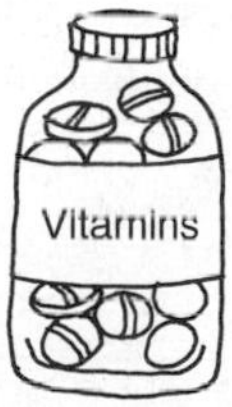

take

5.

get an appointment with

CULTURE NOTE

Chiropractic treatments involve adjusting the spine, usually to relieve pain. For many years, most people didn't believe this could help them. Today there are thousands of chiropractors in the United States. Many insurance plans pay for chiropractic visits.

D. Questions

questions	possible answers	
Would + subject + *like* + noun or infinitive	***Affirmative***	***Negative***
Would you like some dinner?	Yes, please.	No, thank you.
Would you like to go out for lunch?	Yes, of course.	Sorry, but I can't today.

exercise 4

Work with a partner. Ask and answer questions. Use *would you like to . . . ?* with the following cues. Give true answers.

example: learn CPR (cardiopulmonary resuscitation)

A: **Would you like to learn CPR?**
B: **Yes, it's very important.**

1. change your eating habits
2. learn first aid
3. learn how to ski
4. travel around the world
5. open a business someday
6. go back to your country soon

Using What You've Learned

activity 1

Making Requests. Ask other students for something—anything! Go around the room making requests and responding to them. Continue asking until everyone has a turn.

example: A: **Could you help me with my homework?**
B: **Sure I could. Could you give me your credit card?**
C: **Sorry, but I don't have my wallet with me.**

activity 2 **Making Requests.** Work with a partner. Role-play these telephone conversations. Then create one of your own.

1. You want to make a dental appointment for a checkup. Call the dentist's office.
2. You have a bad toothache, and you would like to make an emergency appointment with the dentist. Call the dentist's office.
3. You want to make an appointment with your doctor for a yearly checkup. Call the doctor's office.
4. You need a prescription for antibiotics. Ask the pharmacist.

TOPIC three

Should, must, and have to

Setting the Context

prereading questions Look at the picture. Is this a serious accident? Why is the police officer writing a ticket?

Emergency Situations

A Misha is driving with his daughter, Yuliya. Yuliya is only two years old, but she is not sitting in a car seat. She is not even wearing a seat belt. A car turns in front of Misha, and he has to stop quickly. Yuliya hits her head, but she is not hurt seriously.

B Now the other driver is getting out of his car. What should Misha do? He doesn't know. Then a policewoman stops. She is angry at Misha. "Do you have insurance? You must keep insurance information in your car! Where is your child's car seat? You must not drive without a car seat! You should know this. I am going to give you a ticket."

C Misha is lucky because Yuliya isn't hurt. But Misha is very upset. He will put his insurance information in the car today, and he is going to buy a car seat too.

discussion questions

Circle T (True) or F (False).

1. T F Misha knows all the U.S. driving laws very well.

2. T F Misha needs to buy a car seat for his daughter.

3. T F Misha has to pay money for his mistake.

4. T F Misha is going to keep his birth certificate in his car.

A. Giving Advice

affirmative	negative	notes
Subject + *should* + verb	**Subject + *should not* / *shouldn't* + verb**	
I / You / He / She / It / We / They } **should go** now.	I / You / He / She / It / We / They } **should not stay.** / **shouldn't stay.**	Use *should* and *should not* to give advice. The simple form of a verb follows *should* and other modal auxiliaries.

exercise 1 Underline the uses of *should* in the reading on pages 113 and 114.

exercise 2 What should you do in an emergency? What shouldn't you do? Here is a short test for you. First, complete these sentences with *should* or *shouldn't*. Then, in a small group, compare your answers. Do you all agree? Finally, as a group, write one original sentence for each situation.

1. You are walking down the street, and you see a bad car accident. People are hurt seriously. You ___should___ call for help. You ___should___ call the police or 911, the emergency telephone number in many parts of the United States. You ___shouldn't___ walk away.

Sentence: You should try to help.

2. There is a fire in your apartment building. You _____________ use the elevator. If there is a lot of smoke, you _____________ try to run down the hall. You _____________ try to take all your things with you.

Sentence: ____

3. A pregnant woman _____________ drink alcohol or smoke. She _____________ see a doctor early in her pregnancy. She _____________ continue to exercise.

Sentence: ____

4. Carlos doesn't understand the safety rules for his job. He _____________ ask his supervisor or a friend for a translation. He _____________ pretend to understand because he is embarrassed.

Sentence: ____

5. Lidia has trouble sleeping. She _____________ drink a lot of alcohol before bedtime. She _____ take sleeping pills every night. She _____________ talk to her friends. She _____________ go to a doctor.

Sentence: ____

exercise 3 With a partner, look at the chart about emergency situations below. Read the information and check the important vocabulary. Then change each command to a statement with *should* or *should not*.

example: If possible, check the victim for injuries.

If possible, you should check the victim for injuries.

VOCABULARY

artificial respiration = forcing air into someone who is not breathing

injury = a hurt or wound

rescue = to save someone from danger

unconscious = not awake

victim = someone who is hurt

EMERGENCY FIRST AID

1. Call for medical help immediately. (Dial 911.)
2. If possible, check the victim for injuries.
3. Do not move the victim if it is not necessary.
4. If a rescue is necessary, move a victim quickly and carefully.
5. Check for breathing.
6. Give artificial respiration if necessary.
7. Control bleeding.
8. Do not give food or drink to an unconscious victim.

911 is the phone number people use in emergencies in the United States. If you dial 911, the operator will automatically know your phone number and location. That way, help can be sent to you even if you cannot speak.

B. Expressing Needs or Obligations

affirmative	negative	
Subject + *must* + verb	**Subject + *must not* + verb**	
I / You / He / She / It / We / They } **must be** careful.	I / You / He / She / It / We / They } **must not** do that.	*Must* and *must not* are strong expressions. They show that something is very important or necessary. *Must not* also shows that something is not allowed.

exercise 4

Use the cues below to make sentences with *must* or *must not.* Compare your answers in a small group. Write an original sentence for each situation.

example: keep the building clean

The landlord must keep the building clean.

1. If you rent an apartment, the landlord must or must not do this:
- **a.** keep the building clean
- **b.** provide smoke alarms
- **c.** enter your apartment without your permission
- **d.** make repairs quickly
- **e.** rent to people of any color or religion
- **f.** ______________________________

2. If you drive a car, you must or must not do this:
- **a.** use a car seat for young children
- **b.** bring your license with you
- **c.** keep your car registration and insurance information in the car
- **d.** drive with six or more people in a compact car
- **e.** ______________________________

3. If you have small children, you must or must not do this:
   a. leave them home alone, even for a short time
   b. use car seats for them
   c. leave medicine or cleaning supplies around the house
   d. get immunizations for them
   e. ____

exercise 5 Read this label from a bottle of cold medicine. The label uses difficult vocabulary, but the information is important. Then look at each pair of sentences below. Circle the letter of the sentence with the correct meaning.

All Night Cold Medicine

WARNING: Use this product ONLY as directed. Do not exceed the recommended dosage. Do not use this product for more than seven days. If your condition does not improve, consult a doctor. Do not take this product if you have heart disease or diabetes. Avoid alcoholic beverages while you are taking this product. Use caution when driving a motor vehicle or using machinery.

1. Use this product ONLY as directed.
   a. You must follow the directions for this medicine.
   b. You don't need to read the directions.
2. Do not exceed the recommended dosage.
   a. You can take any amount of medicine.
   b. You must take the correct amount of medicine for your age or weight.
3. Do not use this product for more than seven days.
   a. You must not take this medicine for more than a week.
   b. You must take this medicine for a week.
4. If your condition does not improve, consult a doctor.
   a. If you get better, you should talk to a doctor.
   b. If you do not feel better, you should talk to a doctor.
5. Do not take this product if you have heart disease or diabetes.
   a. If you have heart problems or diabetes, you must not use this medicine.
   b. You must use this medicine if you have heart problems or diabetes.
6. Avoid alcoholic beverages while you are taking this product.
   a. You can take this medicine and drink beer or wine at the same time.
   b. You must not take this medicine and drink beer or wine at the same time.
7. Use caution when driving a motor vehicle or using machinery.
   a. You must be very careful when you are driving or using a machine.
   b. You can drive or use a machine and take this medicine at the same time without any problems.

C. *Have to* and *must*

	examples	notes
have to	You **have to use** a car seat with small children.	In affirmative statements, *have to* and *must* are very similar in meaning.
must	You **must use** a car seat with small children.	

exercise 6 Rewrite the sentences below. Use *have to* or *has to* in each new sentence.

example: Misha must buy a car seat for his daughter.
Misha has to buy a car seat for his daughter.

1. Misha must pay his ticket.

____

2. You must drive carefully at all times.

____

3. You must obey the speed limits.

____

4. Young children must sit in car seats.

____

5. You must read the instructions on medicine bottles.

____

6. Children must have immunizations.

____

7. Your landlord must keep the building clean.

____

8. Your landlord must put smoke alarms in your building.

____

D. *Don't/doesn't have to* Versus *must not*

	examples	notes
don't/doesn't have to	Adults **don't have to use** car seats.	*Don't/doesn't have to* means "It is not necessary."
must not	You **must not drive** without a license.	*Must not* has a very different meaning. *Must not* means "It is not allowed." There is no choice.

exercise 7 Check the correct statements.

example: ☐ You don't have to drink and drive.
☑ You must not drink and drive.

1. ☐ You don't have to carry an umbrella in the rain.
   ☐ You must not carry an umbrella in the rain.
2. ☐ You don't have to put a knife in a toaster.
   ☐ You must not put a knife in a toaster.
3. ☐ You don't have to drive without a seat belt.
   ☐ You must not drive without a seat belt.
4. ☐ You don't have to keep your birth certificate in your car.
   ☐ You must not keep your birth certificate in your car.
5. ☐ You don't have to take the TOEFL to enter some colleges.
   ☐ You must not take the TOEFL to enter some colleges.

Using What You've Learned

activity 1 **Explaining Rules.** It's important to "know the rules" in a new situation. Sometimes there are specific rules or even laws, and we must or must not do some things. Other things are important to do (or not to do), but we have a choice.

Think about the three situations on page 120. Work with a partner and write rules for each situation. Then explain the rules to the class.

	must	should	doesn't have to
1. A visitor to the U.S. or Canada	obey the laws	try to speak the language	carry a birth certificate
2. A student in this program			
3. A visitor to your native country			

examples: **A visitor to the U.S. or Canada must obey the laws.**
A visitor to the U.S. or Canada should try to speak English or French.
A visitor to the U.S. or Canada doesn't have to carry a birth certificate.

activity 2

Talking About Emergency Situations. With a partner or in a small group, talk about first aid in a real situation. Take turns asking and answering these questions.

example: You see and smell a fire in the house next door. What should you do?
You should call the fire department or 911. Then you should get outside quickly.

1. You see a bad car accident. What should you do first?
2. The people in the car have injuries. Should you move them?
3. The car is starting to burn. Should you move the victims?
4. One person is not breathing. Should you try to give the person water? What should you do?
5. One person is bleeding a lot. What should you do?

TOPIC four

Might with Possibilities; Simple Future Tense with will; Using or

Setting the Context

prereading questions

In this picture, a group of friends are playing soccer. What is happening?

Call 911

ALFONSO: Ohhh . . . My leg . . .
FRANK: What's the matter? Are you OK? What hurts?
ALFONSO: My left leg . . . My ankle . . .
ALI: His ankle might be sprained, or it might be broken.
ALVARO: How far is the hospital? Let's take him there.
KEIZO: We shouldn't move him. That might make it worse. I'll call 911 right now.
BEDI: Let's find a phone. It won't take long for someone to come, will it?
ALVARO: Don't worry, Alfonso. You'll be OK. Help will be here in a minute. We'll take good care of you.

discussion questions

1. Who is hurt? Which leg is hurt?
2. Are his friends going to take him to the hospital? If not, what are they going to do?

A. Expressing Present and Future Possibilities

affirmative	negative	notes
Subject + *might* + verb	**Subject + *might not* + verb**	
I / You / He / She / It / We / They } **might stay** here.	I / You / He / She / It / We / They } **might not leave.**	*Might* means "maybe," "perhaps," or "possibly." *Might* is rarely used in questions. The simple form of a verb follows *might* and other modal auxiliaries.

exercise 1 Underline the uses of *might* in the conversation on page 121. Circle the verb after each.

exercise 2 Read these statements, and make statements with *might*. Use the cues in parentheses.

example: It's cloudy today. (rain)
It might rain.

1. It's winter. It's very cold and cloudy. (snow)
2. She isn't in class today. (be sick)
3. He is sick, and he feels hot and cold. (have a fever)
4. She's only eating salad and yogurt. (be on a diet)
5. I never see him eat meat. (be a vegetarian)
6. She cries often. (be homesick)

B. *Or*

	examples	notes
Two Sentences	I might go to the library. I might go shopping.	*Or* can join two sentences. In writing, use a comma (,) before *or.*
One Sentence	I might go to the library, **or** I might go shopping.	

exercise 3 What alternatives are these people thinking about? Make sentences with *might* and *or.*

example: **She might stay on her diet, or she might have an ice-cream cone.**

1.

2.

3.

4.

5.

C. The Simple Future Tense

Subject + *will* + verb	Subject + *will not* / *won't* + verb	
Affirmative	***Negative***	***Notes***
I / You / He / She / It / We / They } **will be** here soon.	I / You / He / She / It / We / They } **will not be** late. **won't be** late.	*Will* is used to talk about the future. People also use *will* to make offers, predictions, promises, and requests.

exercise 4 We often use *will* or *won't* to make promises. Imagine you are a new student at college. You are talking to your parents. Use the following cues to make promises with *will* or *won't*. Then add two more promises.

example: eat healthy food

I promise I will eat healthy food, Mom.

1. eat breakfast every day
2. get a lot of sleep
3. not go to many parties
4. get some exercise every week
5. not watch soap operas
6. read more books
7. do the laundry
8. not call collect
9. ______________
10. ______________

D. Questions and Answers

					Possible Answers
Statement	She will		study for the test.		
Yes/no Questions	***Will*** **+ subject + verb**				
	Will	she	**study** for the test?		Yes, she will. No, she won't.
Information Questions	***Question word* + *Will* + subject + *verb***				
	When	**will**	she	**study?**	Tonight.
	Where	**will**	she	**study?**	At home.

exercise 5 People often use *will* to make requests. Work with a partner. Imagine you are very good friends. Both of you are moving to new places, and you are saying good-bye. Take turns making requests and giving responses. Use the cues below and add two original requests.

example: write soon

A: **Will you write soon?**
B: **Of course. I promise I will.**

1. call me from time to time
2. take care of yourself
3. have a good time
4. be careful
5. remember all of us
6. keep in touch
7. _____
8. _____

exercise 6 Two old friends meet each other on the street. Complete their conversation with the simple present or the simple future tense. Add negatives when indicated.

JANE: Hi, Susan. How ___are___ (be) you? You ___look___ (look) great!

SUSAN: Well, I ___1___ (work) at the health club, and I ___2___ (get) a lot of exercise. I ___3___ (teach) aerobics classes there.

JANE: ___4___ you ___5___ (like) it?

SUSAN: Yes, I ___6___ (like) it very much because my job ___7___ (be) fun, and it ___8___ (keep) me in good shape. It ___9___ (be) a great combination.

JANE: I ___10___ (not get) any exercise, and I ___11___ (need) to change that. I ___12___ (want) to look good—like you! ___13___ you ___14___ (be) there tomorrow? I ___15___ (come) and ___16___ (register) for a class.

SUSAN: Come in the morning. I ___17___ (be) at the club from 8:00 to 11:30, but I ___18___ (not be) there in the afternoon. OK? I ___19___ (see) you tomorrow!

exercise 7 Complete this conversation with *can, can't, could, would, should, must, will,* or *won't.* Use each modal at least once.

JANE: I ___can't___ do this! I ___can't___ exercise anymore.

SUSAN: Yes, you ___1___! You ___2___ try harder!

JANE: ___3___ I stop for a minute? I ___4___ like to die.

SUSAN: ____________ you like to take a break? You know, Jane, you
5
____________ get more exercise. Next time, you ____________ feel
6 7
much better.

JANE: I ____________ be here next time because I ____________ be in the
8 9
hospital!

Using What You've Learned

activity 1

Asking Questions. Work with a partner. Take turns asking and answering these questions. Give true answers. Use *be going to* for specific plans. Use *might* for possible plans. Then add one question each.

example: A: **What are you going to do after class?**
B: **I might go to the library, or I might go home.**
or I am going to go to the library.

STUDENT A

1. What are you going to do tonight?
2. What are you going to wear tomorrow?
3. Where are you going to spend your next vacation?
4. ____

STUDENT B

1. What are you going to have for dinner?
2. Where are you going to go tomorrow night?
3. What are you going to do next weekend?
4. ____

activity 2

GROUP ACTIVITY

Pantomiming. Play this game in a group or as a class. One student thinks of a word. The student acts out the meaning *without speaking.* The other students try to guess the word. Look at the ideas on page 127 and add some of your own. Use *might* in your guesses.

JOBS	ANIMALS	ATHLETES	ILLNESSES OR INJURIES
carpenter	cat	basketball player	the flu
doctor	elephant	golfer	a headache
pilot	lion	soccer player	a stomachache
plumber	tiger	tennis player	a toothache

example: A: **Keizo might be a plumber.**
B: **He might be a carpenter.**
C: **No! I know! He's a doctor.**

activity 3

Making Offers. Make an offer other students cannot refuse! Go around the room in a chain. One student makes an offer. The next student responds and then makes an offer. The third student responds, and so on. Some possible responses are listed below.

example: A: **I'll give you a ride home.**
B: **Great! I'll cook dinner for you tonight.**
C: **No way! . . .**

Possible Responses

	Affirmative	*Negative*
Formal	Thank you very much.	I'm sorry, but . . .
Informal	Thanks a lot! Great! Sure thing!	Thanks, but no thanks. No way! Nothing doing!

activity 4

Making Predictions. Write your name on a piece of paper. Your teacher will collect the papers in a bag. Choose one name, but do not say it out loud. Use *will* or *won't* to write five predictions about that student's future. Your teacher will collect the predictions and then read them aloud. You do not have to sign your name.

example: Abdullah will become famous because he will be the star of an international TV program. He'll be very rich, but he won't forget about us. He'll invite us all to his home in Beverly Hills.

checking your progress

Check your progress with structures from Chapters Three and Four. Be sure to review any problem areas.

Part 1: Choose the correct word(s) to complete each sentence.

1. I _____ a problem.
   a. has
   b. are
   c. have
   d. having

2. Sue _____ the dishes at night.
   a. does
   b. do
   c. doing
   d. is

3. Penny _____.
   a. cant sleep
   b. can't sleeps
   c. can't sleep
   d. canot sleep

4. Who _____ the house?
   a. does cleans
   b. does clean
   c. cleans
   d. clean

5. Marina usually _____ cook.
   a. doesn't
   b. do not
   c. don't
   d. not

6. Could you _____ me please?
   a. help
   b. help me
   c. helps
   d. helping

7. I would _____.
   a. like to come
   b. to come
   c. liked to come
   d. like to came

8. Every night Joe _____ eight hours.
   a. is sleeping
   b. is slept
   c. sleep
   d. sleeps

9. I _____ hot dogs.
   a. hate
   b. am hating
   c. hates
   d. am

10. Misha has _____ for his ticket.
    a. to pay
    b. pays
    c. to paid
    d. not paying

Part 2: Circle the correct words to complete this story. Circle "X" to show that nothing is necessary.

My family is very important to me. (Mine / My)[1] mother died three years ago, but my father and two brothers (live / are live)[2] together in Mexico. I'm in the U.S. now, but we stay in touch. My father (calls / call)[3] me almost every weekend. My brothers and I write each other on e-mail.

My dad (has / is)[4] 65 years old. He is still (working / works)[5] as a doctor. He should (retires / retire)[6] soon. My older brother owns his own restaurant. He (usually works / works usually)[7] six nights a week. My younger brother is still in high school. He (hates / is hating)[8] to study, though. He would like (to spend / spend)[9] all his time at parties. He (should / might)[10] fail his classes. He is very smart, so he (must not / doesn't have to)[11] study very hard. But, he (have to / has to)[12] study a little!

E-mail or electronic mail is a way of sending messages from one computer to another. Today several million people use e-mail instead of sending letters through regular mail because it's less expensive and much faster.

CHAPTER five

Men and Women

in this chapter

The Simple Past Tense

Topic One:	Simple Past Tense of the Verb *be;* Yes/No Questions; Information Questions; *there was/were*
Topic Two:	Simple Past Tense with Regular Verbs; Spelling and Pronunciation; Affirmative and Negative Statements; Yes/No and Wh Questions
Topic Three:	*So, had to, could*
Topic Four:	Review of Chapters One through Five

TOPIC **one**

Simple Past Tense of the Verb *be*; Yes/No Questions; Information Questions; *there was / were*

Setting the context

prereading questions

Look at the pictures on page 133. What are they comparing?

The Good Old Days

A I'm a very old man now, and things change. When I was young, everything was different. There weren't so many decisions to make. We were not as free as young people today. But there weren't as many problems. In a way, life was easier.

B Take marriage, for example. Who were you going to marry? It was simple. Just ask your parents. They were happy to find a wife for you.

C Of course, you could look for a wife yourself. But you and she couldn't just decide to marry. You had to ask your father and her father. They could say yes or no. They could decide. We couldn't.

D You see? Everything was different.

discussion questions

Circle T (True) or F (False). Then correct the false sentences.

1. T (F) In the past, everything was ~~the same~~ different.

2. T F You could look for a wife.

3. T F You and she could decide to marry.

4. T F You had to ask your mother and her mother.

5. T F The fathers could say yes or no to the marriage.

A. *Was* and *Were*—Affirmative and Negative Statements

affirmative	negative: Long Form	negative: Contraction
I **was** happy.	I **was not** sad.	I **wasn't** sad.
You **were** happy.	You **were not** sad.	You **weren't** sad.
He / She / It **was** happy.	He / She / It **was not** sad.	He / She / It **wasn't** sad.
We / You / They **were** happy.	We / You / They **were not** sad.	We / You / They **weren't** sad.

I'm Christine. The man in the reading was my grandfather. To show you how things have changed in our culture, I'd like to tell you a little about my family history.

1. My parents <u>were</u> introduced in 1938. They _____ at a dance.

2. My mother's name _____ Catherine. My father's _____ Robert.

3. My father _____ a medical student. My mother _____ in high school.

4. My mother _____ quite young. She _____ eighteen. My father _____ (not) as young. He _____ twenty-five.

5. They _____ (not) from the same city. My father _____ from Philadelphia. My mother _____ from New York.

6. They _____ also from different backgrounds. My father's family _____ Scandinavian. My mother's _____ from Spain.

7. Even their religion _____ (not) the same. My father _____ a Protestant. My mother _____ a Catholic.*

8. Finally, her family _____ rich. His family _____ poor.

9. To them, these things _____ (not) important. They _____ in love!

*There are many types of Christians. Two major groups are Protestants and Catholics.

B. *Was* and *Were*—Yes/No Questions and Short Answers

questions	short answers: Affirmative	short answers: Negative
Was or were **+ subject**		
Was I tired?	Yes, I **was.** (You **were.**)	No, I **wasn't.**
Were you late?	Yes, you **were.** (I **was.**)	No, you **weren't.** (I **wasn't.**)
Was {he / she / it} late?	Yes, {he / she / it} **was.**	No, {he / she / it} **wasn't.**
Were {we / you / they} hungry?	Yes, {we / you / they} **were.**	No, {we / you / they} **weren't.**

exercise 2 Work with a partner. Ask and answer these questions about exercise 1.

example: A: **Were Catherine and Robert introduced at school?**

B: **No, they weren't.**

1. Was Robert a medical student?
2. Were they from different backgrounds?
3. Was Catherine the same age as Robert?
4. Were they from the same city?
5. Was Robert from Philadelphia?
6. Was Catherine from Los Angeles?

exercise 3 How about your parents? Use questions 2–4 in exercise 2, but change the names to *your mother* and *your father.* Work with a partner. Take turns asking and answering your new questions. Then make two more questions. Ask your partner these new questions.

C. Information Questions with *who*

	examples	notes
Statement	Catherine's parents were from Spain.	
Yes/No Question	***Was* or *were* + subject** **Were** Catherine's parents from Spain?	
Question with who	***Who* + *was* + adjective, noun, or phrase** **Who was** from Spain?	Questions with *who* are normally singular.

D. Information Questions with *when, where, how long,* and *how old*

	examples	possible answers:
Statement	They were married in New York in 1941.	
Yes/No Question	***Was* or *were* + subject** **Were** they married in New York in 1941?	Yes, they were.
Information Question	**Question word + *was* or *were* + subject** **When were** they married? **Where were** they married?	In 1941. In New York.

exercise 4 Make questions from the statements on page 137. The answers to the questions are the underlined words.

examples: Robert was a medical student.
Who was a medical student?
They were introduced in 1938.
When were they introduced?

1. Robert and Catherine were at a dance.
2. Robert was from Philadelphia.
3. Catherine was from New York.
4. She was eighteen.
5. He was twenty-five.
6. Robert's parents were Scandinavian.
7. Her family was from Spain.
8. He was a Protestant.
9. She was a Catholic.
10. They were married in 1939.

CULTURE NOTE

Marriage between two people of different religions or cultural backgrounds was once unusual in the United States. Today, such marriages are more common. How common are these types of marriages in your culture?

E. *There was / were*—Statements and Questions

	affirmative statements	negative statements
With a Singular Noun	**There was** a problem.	**There wasn't** a problem.
With Plural Nouns	**There were** some problems.	**There weren't** many problems.

	yes/no questions	possible answers: *Affirmative*	possible answers: *Negative*
With a Singular Noun	**Was there** a problem?	Yes, **there was.**	No, **there wasn't.**
With Plural Nouns	**Were there** many problems?	Yes, **there were.**	No, **there weren't.**

exercise 5 Use *was* or *were* to complete these sentences. Use contractions for the negatives.

1. The marriage was a bad idea. There were several reasons.
2. First, there _____ religious differences between Catherine and Robert.
3. There _____ problems with money.
4. There _____ (not) many jobs at that time.
5. There _____ even a bigger problem.
6. There _____ a huge war in Europe.
7. In the U.S., there _____ many young men already in the military.
8. There _____ (not) much hope for an end to the war.

CULTURE NOTE

In past wars (for example, in World War II, Korea, and Vietnam), the U.S. government used a draft system to choose young men for the military. Today, there is no draft: The U.S. military is all volunteers. Is there a military draft in your country?

Using What You've Learned

activity **Asking About Family Histories.** Do you know about your family history? Work with a new partner. Take turns asking and answering questions about your parents. Use these cues to make questions. Then add some of your own. Take notes and write a short paragraph about your partner's family.

examples: parents / born in the same city
Were your parents born in the same city?
where / born
Where were they born?

1. when / born
2. rich or poor
3. when / married
4. how old
5. mother younger than your father

TOPIC two

Simple Past Tense with Regular Verbs—Spelling and Pronunciation; Affirmative and Negative Statements; Questions

Setting the Context

prereading questions These pictures are from the 1940s during World War II. How did the war change people's lives?

Spoils of War

A In 1941, my father and millions of other men went to war. At the same time, my mother and millions of other women went to work.

B The United States needed many things. We needed ships, tanks, guns, and other equipment. Who stayed in the country and made these things? Women did. They did the work in factories and offices. They helped build everything from tanks to houses. They were workers; they were supervisors. They won the war just as much as the men did.

C When the war was over, many women did not want to go back to their places in the home. I know my mother didn't. In this way, World War II changed the relationship between men and women in the United States.

discussion questions

1. What did many men do during World War II?
2. What did many women do?
3. What happened to women after World War II?

A. Simple Past Tense of Regular Verbs—Affirmative Statements

Subject + verb + -ed

singular		***plural***		***notes***
I You He She It	**worked.**	We You They	**worked.**	The simple past tense is used to talk about actions or situations in the past. This chapter focuses on regular verbs. These verbs use the *-ed* ending.

B. Pronunciation

The *-ed* ending has three different pronunciations:

- /t/ after voiceless sounds such as /p/ and /k/
- /d/ after voiced sounds such as /v/ and /g/
- /id/ after /t/ and /d/

/t/	***/d/***	***/id/***
helped	arrived	needed
watched	cleaned	started
worked	hugged	waited

Do you know the meanings of all the verbs in the list below? Underline any you don't know. Discuss them with your teacher. Then work with a partner. Practice the different sounds of the *-ed* ending. You say one of the verbs, and your partner says the past form of that verb.

/t/		/d/		/id/	
fix	talk	arrive	learn	fold	paint
help	wash	clean	listen	hate	start
kiss	watch	enter	love	invite	visit
like	work	hug	return	lift	wait
miss		join	stay	need	want

exercise 2

Use these pictures and cues to make sentences. Use the past tense of the verbs.

clean	iron	watch
fix	listen to	wash
fold	✓ stay	

example: **Before World War II, most women stayed at home.**

at home

1.

the clothes

2.

the clothes

3.

the clothes

4.

the house

5.

the children

6.

the meals

7.

yes, dear.

their husbands

C. Spelling

words ending in consonant + *y*		words ending in vowel + *y*		
study	studied	enjoy	enjoyed	For verbs ending with consonant + *y*, change *y* to *i* and add *-ed*. Verbs ending with vowel + *y* add *-ed* only.
try	tried	play	played	

one vowel + one consonant		one vowel + *w* or *x*		
hug	hugged	fix	fixed	For most verbs ending with one vowel and one consonant, double the final consonant and add *-ed*. For verbs ending with vowel + *w* or *x*, add *-ed* only.
plan	planned	sew	sewed	
shop	shopped			

Common Exceptions

enter	entered	open	opened
happen	happened	travel	traveled
iron	ironed	visit	visited
listen	listened		

Note: For verbs ending in *e*, add *-d* only: *arrived—arrived.*

exercise 3 Complete each group of sentences with the verbs listed. Use the simple past tense.

1. *change* During the war, the situation changed.
2. *hug, join, kiss, start* Men __________ the military. Women __________ and __________ their husbands good-bye. Then women __________ to work.
3. *clean, stay, watch* Before the war, most women __________ at home. They __________ the house and __________ the children.
4. *fix, fold, wash* They __________ and __________ the clothes. Then they __________ the meals.
5. *help, need, work* During the war, the country __________ workers. Many women __________ in industry. They __________ build things for the war.

6. *learn, like, work* Christine's mother __________ in a factory from 1941 to 1946. She __________ to build cars. The work was difficult, but she __________ it.

7. *listen, stay, talk, wait* On weekends, Christine's mom usually __________ at home. She __________ to the radio and __________ for letters to come. She also __________ to friends on the phone.

8. *arrive, join, stay* Christine's father __________ the navy in 1941. He __________ in North Africa two years later. He __________ in the navy for five years.

9. *end, hate, love, return* Robert was a doctor. He __________ his work, but he __________ the navy. The war finally __________ in 1946. Then Robert __________ home.

D. Negative Statements

long form	contraction
Subject + *did* + *not* + verb	**Subject + *didn't* + verb**
I / You / He / She / It / We / You / They } **did not work.**	I / You / He / She / It / We / You / They } **didn't go.**

exercise 4 Read the information about Christine's father. The sentences that follow are not correct. Correct the sentences as in the examples.

Name: Robert L. Nathanson

Eye Color: blue

Hair Color: brown

Height: 6'2"*

Weight: 180 lbs.†

Birth Date: February 15, 1913

Branch of Service: navy

Length of Service: 1941–1946

Rank: captain

Job: surgeon

Awards: 3 for bravery

Attitude: hated the military

Area Served In: North Africa

examples: Robert joined the army.
Robert didn't join the army. He joined the navy.
He was in Europe.
He wasn't in Europe. He was in North Africa.

1. Robert worked as a pilot.
2. He served for nine years.
3. He received twelve awards.
4. He was a general.
5. He loved the military.
6. He had brown eyes and blue hair.
7. He was five feet two inches.
8. He weighed 210 pounds.

**6'2"* six feet two inches
†*lbs.* the abbreviation for pounds

E. Yes/No Questions and Short Answers

questions	short answers	
***Did* + subject + verb**	***Affirmative***	***Negative***
Did { I / you / he / she / it / we / you / they } **work?**	Yes, { I / you / he / she / it / we / you / they } **did.**	No, { I / you / he / she / it / we / you / they } **didn't.**

***exercise* 5** Read the information about Christine's mother. Then work with a partner. One student uses the eight sentences on page 146 to make yes/no questions. The other student answers the questions. Then change roles.

Name of Employee: Catherine Nathanson
Residence: 2109 Hillside Drive, Queens, New York
Telephone: 724-2686
Marital Status: married
Maiden Name: Molina
Children: none
Eye Color: brown
Hair Color: brown
Height: 5'4"
Weight: 110 lbs.
Birth Date: May 28, 1920
Job: welder*
Work Experience: none
Attitude: works very hard
enjoys her job

General Automobiles Incorporated

**welder* a person who uses heat to join pieces of metal

examples: Catherine worked in an automobile plant.

A: **Did Catherine work in an automobile plant?**
B: **Yes, she did.**

She was a welder.

B: **Was she an engineer?**
A: **No, she wasn't.**

1. My mother had a lot of experience.
2. She had brown hair and brown eyes.
3. She weighed 210 pounds.
4. My mother was married.
5. My mother had children.
6. She liked her job.
7. She was eighteen years old.
8. She lived in New York.

F. Subject Questions with *who* or *what*

	examples	notes
Statement	My father had an accident.	To ask about a subject, use *who* or *what* + past tense verb. Do not use *did* in these questions.
Question with who	***Who* + past tense verb** **Who had** an accident?	
Statement	An accident happened last night.	
Question with what	***What* + past tense verb** **What happened** last night?	

G. Information Questions

Statements	I studied English at the library from eight to ten every night. She studied French with her roommate on weekends.	
Yes/No Questions and Possible Answers	***Did* + subject + verb** **Did** you **study** every night? **Did** she **study** every night?	 Yes, I did. Yes, she did.
Information Questions and Possible Answers	**Question word + *Did* + subject + verb** **How often did** you **study?** **How long did** you **study?** **What did** you **study?** **Where did** you **study?** **When did** she **study?** **What did** she **study?** **Who* did** she **study** with?	 Every night. Two hours. English. At the library. On weekends. French. With her roommate.

*In formal English, *whom* is used for these questions.

exercise 6 Here is some more information about Robert's experience in the navy. For each sentence, make questions about the underlined words.

example: The U.S. entered the war in 1941.
When did the U.S. enter the war?

1. My dad joined the navy.
2. He was in the navy for five years.
3. He was a surgeon.
4. He helped injured soldiers.
5. He worked in a hospital.
6. The work was difficult but interesting.
7. He enjoyed his work.
8. The navy was terrible.
9. He hated the navy.
10. He missed my mom.
11. He wrote to my mom almost every night.
12. The war lasted for four long years.

Using What You've Learned

activity 1

Playing a Guessing Game. Do you know the game Twenty Questions? Pretend you are a famous person who is dead. Other students have to guess your name. They can ask you questions in the past tense, but you can only answer yes or no.

activity 2

GROUP ACTIVITY

Telling Stories. In small groups, tell about life in your countries fifty years ago. What was a typical woman's life like? What was a typical man's life like?

Then tell about life in your country today. What is a woman's life like today? What is a man's life like? Are men's and women's roles changing?

After you tell about life in your country, past and present, use your ideas to write a short composition.

TOPIC three

So, had to, could

Setting the Context

prereading questions

Did your mother work outside the house when you were growing up? How about now? Today in your country, do most women work in the house or have jobs outside?

Working in Wartime

During the war, my mom's life changed completely. My father was gone, so she couldn't depend on him to earn money. She had to earn enough money to support herself. When she started working, it was very difficult, so she didn't like it. But, after a while, she realized that she could do the work as well as or even better than most men. Then, she really began to enjoy her work.

discussion questions

1. Why did Christine's mother have to earn money?
2. Did she like her job at first?
3. What did she realize after a while?
4. When did she begin to enjoy her work?

A. So

	examples	possible answers:
Two Sentences	Catherine and Robert didn't have much money. They couldn't buy a car.	*So* means "as a result." *So* can join two sentences. A comma (,) is used before *so*.
One Sentence	Catherine and Robert didn't have much money**, so** they couldn't buy a car.	

exercise 1 Omit *because* and use *so* in the following sentences. Add commas and make other necessary changes.

example: My mother couldn't drive to work because she didn't have a car.
My mother didn't have a car, so she couldn't drive to work.

1. My mother used the bus because she didn't have a car.
2. The ride to work was over an hour because the bus was very slow.
3. She worked eleven hours a day because there was a lot of work to do.
4. She worked extra hours because she needed the money.
5. She didn't like the job at first because it was very difficult.
6. Later she liked the work more because she became good at welding.
7. She sometimes felt very lonely because no one lived with her.
8. She decided to live alone because she wanted to be independent.

exercise 2 Match the sentences in Column A with the sentences in Column B. Then join the sentences with *so*. Remember to change punctuation. The first one is done for you. (See top of page 151.)

COLUMN A	COLUMN B
1. There was a war.	**a.** He helped save lives.
2. My mother was lonely.	**b.** She helped build cars.
3. My dad hated the navy.	**c.** My father had to leave home.
4. My mother worked for a car company.	**d.** He wanted to come home as soon as possible.
5. My father was a surgeon.	**e.** She started to make more money.
6. The navy needed surgeons.	**f.** She bought a used car.
7. My mom became a supervisor.	**g.** She wrote to my father a lot.
8. My mother was tired of taking the bus.	**h.** The navy asked my dad to stay.

1. There was a war, so my father had to leave home.

2. ______________________________

3. ______________________________

4. ______________________________

5. ______________________________

6. ______________________________

7. ______________________________

8. ______________________________

exercise 3 Use your imagination and the word *so* to complete the following sentences.

example: My parents fell in love, so they got married.

1. My mom worked very hard as a welder, ______________________________.
2. She became very good at her job, ______________________________.
3. My father joined the navy, ______________________________.
4. He had to work very long hours, ______________________________.
5. It is very hot, ______________________________.
6. It's late and I'm tired, ______________________________.

B. Expressing Past Abilities with *could*—Statements and Questions

affirmative	negative	notes
Subject + *could* + verb	**Subject + *couldn't* / *could not* + verb**	
I / You / He / She / It / We / They **could work.**	I / You / He / She / It / We / They **couldn't work.** / **could not work.**	*Could* and *couldn't* (*could not*) are used to talk about past abilities. The simple form of a verb always follows *could, couldn't,* and other modal auxiliaries.

yes/no questions	possible answers	
***Could* + subject + verb**	***Affirmative***	***Negative***
Could I / you / he / she / it / we / you / they **work?**	Yes, I / you / he / she / it / we / you / they **could.**	No, I / you / he / she / it / we / you / they **couldn't.**

***exercise* 4**

Use *could* or *couldn't (could not)* to complete these sentences about the United States.

1. Before World War II, women __could__ work in offices. They __couldn't__ work in many factories.

2. Women ________ be nurses. Most women ________ be doctors.

3. Women ________ work for large companies. Most of them ________ be executives.

4. Women _______ drive cars. They _______ drive buses.

5. Most women _______ only wear dresses to work. They _______ wear pants.

6. A woman _______ vote. She _______ hope to become President.

> **CULTURE NOTE**
>
> **Since World War II, many women have been working outside the home. In the United States, women usually make less money than men, even when they have the same job. Do many women in your country work outside the home? Do women usually make less money than men?**

C. Expressing Past Needs with *had to*

Subject + *had* + *to* + verb

singular		plural		notes
I You He She It	**had to** study.	We You They	**had to** study.	*Had to* + verb is used to talk about needs or obligations in the past.

exercise 5 World War II ended in 1945, and Christine's father came home. He and Christine's mother had to do many things when he returned. Use *had to* and the cues to make complete sentences. Then, use your imagination to add ideas to the list.

example: they / get to know each other again

They had to get to know each other again.

1. they / learn to live together
2. he / find a new job
3. they / visit many relatives
4. they / decide about having children
5. ______________________________
6. ______________________________

Using What You've Learned

activity 1

GROUP ACTIVITY

Comparing Past and Present Abilities. On your own paper, make a list of at least five things women (or men) can do today that they couldn't do in the past. Make sentences with *can* and *couldn't.*Then, with a partner or in a small group, compare your sentences and share your ideas.

example: drive buses

Women can drive buses today, but they couldn't (do that) twenty years ago.

activity 2

GROUP ACTIVITY

Comparing Past and Present Situations. Compare your life in the past to your life today. Use this chart, and try to make a list of five items for each category. Then make complete sentences. Finally, with a partner or in a small group, compare your experiences. Begin by telling about your past situation: (Five) years ago, I was (wasn't) . . . Then tell about your present situation: Today I am (not) . . .

example: Five years ago, I was in Taiwan. I had to work, so I couldn't go to school everyday.

had to do	could do	couldn't do	can do	can't do
1. work		go to school		
2.				
3.				
4.				
5.				

TOPIC four

Review of Chapters One through Five

Setting the Context

prereading questions

Is there anything unusual in the picture? Do women usually have these types of jobs in your country?

Women's Work

A Hi! This is Christine again. The war finally ended in 1945. During the next years, two great things happened—my dad came home, and I was born! I was the first child, but I wasn't alone for long. In the next four years, my mother had two boys.

B It was great having brothers! The three of us were pretty close in age, so we played together all the time. Our favorite game was cops and robbers. It's funny. Everybody always wanted to be a robber. Of course, someone had to be the cop, and it was usually me.

C Well, I am an adult now, and I'm married, but I still love cops and robbers. Except there's one big difference. I'm a real police officer, so it's not a game anymore.

discussion questions

Circle T (True) or F (False). Correct the false sentences.

1. T F Christine wasn't the first child.
2. T F She has two brothers and one sister.
3. T F Their favorite game was basketball.
4. T F Christine wanted to be a robber.
5. T F Today she is a police officer.

exercise 1 Add the correct form of the verb, and add prepositions where needed.

It's hard to be a police officer, but it's never boring! Just last month there was a mugging* near the police station.

1. The mugging happened (happen) on a Saturday _____ the summer.
2. In fact, it _____ (be) late _____ night _____ July 17, 1992.
3. Two tourists _____ (be) _____ the sidewalk _____ 11:30 P.M.
4. They _____ (have) a lot of money _____ their pockets.
5. Two muggers _____ (be) there _____ the same time.
6. They _____ (have) guns _____ their hands.
7. The muggers _____ (rob) the tourists.
8. The tourists _____ (walk) into the police station _____ midnight.
9. I talked _____ them for thirty minutes, _____ 12:00 A.M. _____ 12:30 A.M.
10. _____ the morning, I _____ (be) able to catch the muggers.
11. Their trial _____ (be) _____ August.
12. They _____ (be) in prison _____ two _____ four years.

exercise 2 Pretend you are a police officer. There was a bank robbery a few minutes ago. You just arrived at the bank. Use the underlined words as cues to make questions from these sentences.

examples: I saw the robbery.
Who saw the robbery?
I saw everything.
What did you see?

1. The robbery happened at 10:30 A.M.
2. A man with long, blond hair walked in the front door.
3. He was about twenty years old.
4. He talked to a teller.†
5. He handed her a note.
6. The note said, "Give me all your money!"
7. He showed her his gun.
8. The teller gave him the money.

**mugging* a robbery that happens to a person on the street
† *teller* a bank employee who works behind a counter

exercise 3

Correct the prepositions in these sentences. In some cases, more than one preposition may be correct.

1. The demonstrators are walking ~~on top of~~ under the bridge.
2. The man with a camera is standing above the bridge.
3. The police are far from the demonstration.
4. A demonstrator is under the police car.
5. The police car is in back of the demonstration.
6. The helicopter is flying on top of the demonstration.
7. Christine is far from the man with a camera.
8. A policeman is standing under two horses.
9. The people with the banner are walking over each other.
10. A dog is standing above the man with a camera.

exercise 4

Join each pair of sentences on page 158 with *because, so,* or *but.*

example: My brothers are not policemen. They all have interesting lives.
My brothers are not policemen, but they have interesting lives.

Robert

1. Robert started college. He couldn't finish.
2. He couldn't finish college. He didn't have enough money.
3. He didn't have enough money. He started looking for a job.
4. Now he makes a lot of money. He doesn't like his job.
5. He doesn't like his job. He has to work a lot.
6. He has to work a lot. He is often very tired.
7. He has to work a lot. There is a lot of work to do.

John

8. John joined the air force. He wanted to fly planes.
9. He joined the air force. He did not become a pilot.
10. His eyes are very bad. He could not learn to fly.
11. He tried new glasses. The glasses didn't help.
12. He wanted to be a pilot. He became a computer operator.
13. He loves his job. He is going to keep doing it.
14. He loves his job. He still wants to be a pilot.

exercise 5

Use pronouns to complete the dialogues. Use subject pronouns *(I, you, he, she, it, we, they),* object pronouns *(me, you, him, her, it, us, them)* or possessives *(my, your, his, her, our, their).*

1. A: Do you know Christine?

   B: Yes, _____ do. I know _____ very well. _____ is a police officer.
2. A: Did you know John and his wife are getting divorced?

   B: Yes, _____ did. I talked to _____ last week. _____ are both pretty depressed.
3. A: You're married. What does _____ wife do?

   B: _____ wife's a bus driver. What about _____ wife?
4. A: Did you and Robert go to the movie?

   B: No, _____ didn't. Both of _____ were too busy.
5. A: We just bought a new house. _____ house is beautiful!

   B: I'd love to see _____.
6. A: Did Christine catch the mugger?

   B: Yes, _____ did. She caught _____ in July.

7. A: Did you know Christine got a new car?

B: Yes, _____ 's black and white. You have a new car too, don't _____ ?

A: Right, but _____ 's purple.

8. A: Are Tony and Ana going to get married?

B: _____ 'm not sure, but I see _____ together a lot.

9. A: I have two children. _____ children are four and six.

B: Mike and Susan have two children too.

A: How old are _____ children?

10. A: Are you going to find a new job?

B: _____ might. My job now bores _____ .

11 A: Are Robert and John going to finish college?

B: No, _____ aren't. School is difficult for _____ .

12. A: We just bought two new bicycles. _____ new bicycles are red.

B: Mike and Susan also have new bikes, but _____ bikes are blue.

exercise 6

Complete this reading in the correct verb tense. Use the past, present, present continuous, and future tenses.

My name __is__ (be) Richard. I ___1___ (be) Christine's husband.

Christine and I ___2___ (be) introduced in college twenty-three years ago. She ___3___ (be) a police science student. I ___4___ (be) an engineering student. After a while, we ___5___ (start) going out on dates. Pretty soon we ___6___ (be) in love.

Well, I ___7___ (not finish) college. After two years, I ___8___ (drop out*). Christine ___9___ (not drop out). She ___10___ (receive) her degree after four years. We ___11___ (be) married after she ___12___ (graduate). In 1975, we ___13___ (move) to Houston.

Now we ___14___ (live) near Houston. Both of us ___15___ (work). She ___16___ (have) a job with the police department. I ___17___ (work) for a department store.

---

* *drop out* to leave school before finishing: *Richard dropped out of school and started working.*

Christine _____ (like) her job more than I like mine. She also _____ (make) more money. I _____ (want) to go back to school. But I _____ (be) just too old! Next year I _____ (look) for another job.
(18) (19) (20) (21) (22)

exercise 7 Complete this reading with *can, must,* or *have to.* In some cases, more than one answer is correct.

When I was a child, I didn't have much freedom. We give our daughter, Marisa, a lot more freedom than I had. For example, she _____ (1) go to friends' homes after school. She _____ (2) go out on dates. She _____ (3) use our car in the day or at night.

She also has a lot of responsibilities. For example, she _____ (4) cook dinner twice a week. She _____ (5) do the dishes four times a week. She _____ (6) help clean the house. She _____ (7) finish all her homework.

Using What You've Learned

activity 1 **Making Rules.** Work with a partner. Imagine that you and your partner are the parents of twins. One of your twins is a boy; the other is a girl. They are both seventeen years old. Give each child a name and then make a list of rules that each child must follow. List at least ten rules. Use the following modal verbs: *must, have to, can, can't, should, shouldn't.*

1. ____________________
2. ____________________
3. ____________________
4. ____________________
5. ____________________
6. ____________________
7. ____________________
8. ____________________
9. ____________________
10. ____________________

activity 2 **Reporting a Robbery.** Work with a partner. You are a police officer. Your partner manages a department store. The store was robbed two hours ago. Ask your partner at least five questions about the robbery. Finally, describe the robbery to the class.

activity 3 **Talking About Your Life.** In Exercise 6, Richard talks about his life. Begin by talking to a partner about your life. What did you do in the past? What about now? What are your plans for the future? Finally, write a short essay about your life. Begin by introducing yourself. Then talk about your past, your present, and your future. Try to use the following verb tenses at least once: simple past, simple present, present continuous, and simple future.

CHAPTER six

Native Americans and Immigrants

in this chapter

The Simple Past Tense with Irregular Verbs

Topic One: Simple Past Tense with Some Irregular Verbs; *too* and *either*

Topic Two: More Irregular Verbs; Tag Questions

Topic Three: More Irregular Verbs; *even though; used to*

Topic Four: More Irregular Verbs; Reported Speech

TOPIC one

Simple Past Tense with Some Irregular Verbs; too and either

Setting the Context

prereading questions

Look at the map. Do you know how Asians first reached North America?

The First Immigrants

A Was Christopher Columbus the first to come to America? Was Leif Ericson? In fact, Columbus wasn't the first, and Ericson wasn't either. People from northern Asia came to America about thirty thousand years before anyone else. Today, we call these people Native Americans, or Indians.

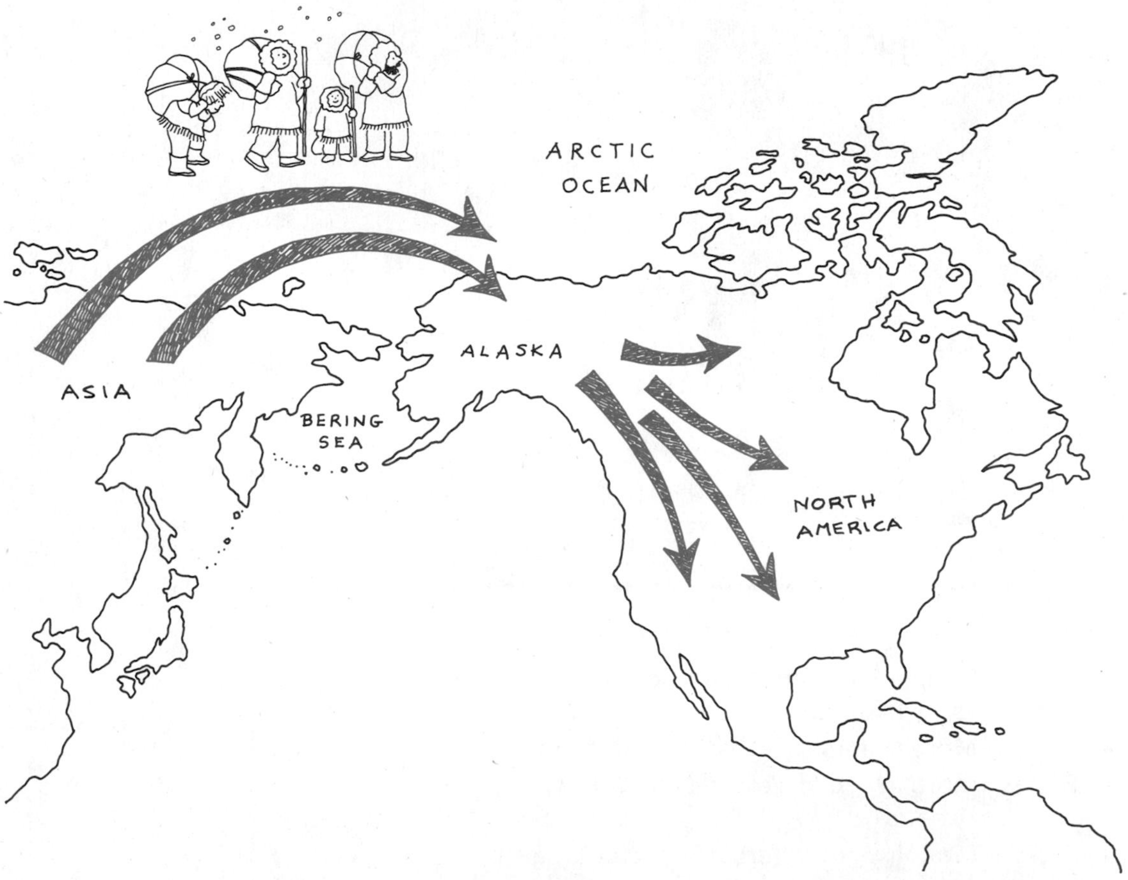

B The Indians came to America because the weather began to change. Northern Asia became very cold. Everything froze. They had to move or die.

C The first Europeans traveled to America in sailboats, but there were no sailboats thirty-thousand years ago. How did the first Indians come to America? They walked!

discussion questions

Circle T (True) or F (False). Correct the false sentences.

1. T F Columbus discovered America first.
2. T F Ericson came to America first.
3. T F It became cold thirty-thousand years ago.
4. T F Everything froze.
5. T F The Indians sailed to America.

A. Irregular Verbs

simple form	past tense form	notes
become	became	Some verbs do not use *-ed* in the past form. These are called irregular verbs. Here are six irregular verbs. There are many others. For a more complete list, see pages 308–309.
begin	began	
come	came	
do	did	
eat	ate	
freeze	froze	
go	went	

exercise 1

Complete these sentences. Use the simple past tense of the verbs in parentheses.

1. The water in the lakes ___froze___ (freeze) last winter.
2. The water in the rivers ___didn't freeze___ (not freeze) last winter.
3. The weather ______________ (begin) to change about thirty thousand years ago.
4. The weather ______________ (not begin) to change last year.
5. It ______________ (become) very cold.
6. It ______________ (not become) very warm.
7. The oceans ______________ (freeze) thirty thousand years ago.
8. The oceans ______________ (not freeze) last year.

9. The people of northern Asia ______________ (eat) meat.

10. The people of northern Asia ______________ (not eat) rice.

11. Some of the people from northern Asia ______________ (go) to America.

12. Some of them ______________ (not go) to America.

exercise 2 Use the past tense to complete the sentences. Then answer the questions in complete sentences.

Caribou

1. Thirty thousand years ago, there ___weren't___ (not be) any people in America. However, there ______________(1) (be) people in northeastern Asia. They ______________(2) (be) hunters. They ______________(3) (eat) caribou.

   a. Were there people in America thirty thousand years ago?
   ___No there weren't___

   b. Were there people in northeastern Asia? ______________

   c. What did they eat? ______________

2. Slowly the weather ______________(1) (begin) to change. It ______________(2) (become) extremely cold. In fact, everything ______________(3) (freeze). The caribou usually ______________(4) (eat)

grass. But the grass ______5______ (freeze). The caribou ______6______ (have) nothing to eat.

a. What began to change? ____________________

b. What did the caribou usually eat? ____________________

c. What happened to the grass? ____________________

3. The weather ______1______ (begin) to get colder and colder. Even part of the ocean between Asia and America ______2______ (freeze). In other words, the ocean ______3______ (become) ice. This new ice ______4______ (become) an ice bridge between the two continents. (See page 164.)

a. What happened to the ocean between Asia and America? ____________________

b. What did this new ice become? ____________________

4. Some caribou ______1______ (go) across this bridge. They ______2______ (come) to Alaska. The hunters ______3______ (come) after them. These hunters ______4______ (walk) from Asia to America. They ______5______ (be) the first Indians.

a. Where did some caribou go? ____________________

b. Who came after the caribou? Why? ____________________

5. Many thousands of Indians probably ______1______ (come) to America on the ice bridge. They ______2______ (go) to all parts of the continent. They divided into hundreds of small nations or tribes. Two important tribes ______3______ (be) the Creek and the Cherokee.

a. How many Indians probably came to America? ____________________

b. Where did they go on the continent? ____________________

c. Did they divide? ____________________

B. *too* with Short Statements

long form	short form	notes
The Creek hunted, and the Cherokee hunted.	The Creek hunted, and the Cherokee **did too**.	When *and* joins two affirmative statements, *too* is sometimes used to make the second statement shorter. The second statement usually has an auxiliary (not a main) verb.
David rides horses all day, and John rides horses all day.	David rides horses all day, and John **does too**.	
I can answer the question, and you can answer the question.	I can answer the question, and you **can too**.	

C. *Using either* with Short Statements

long form	short form	notes
The Cherokee didn't farm, and the Creek didn't farm.	The Cherokee didn't farm, and the Creek **didn't either.**	When *and* joins two negative statements, use *either* instead of *too.* The second statement usually has an auxiliary (not a main) verb.
I'm not tired of grammar, and she isn't tired of grammar.	I'm not tired of grammar, and she **isn't either.**	
They won't be late, and we won't be late.	They won't be late, and we **won't either.**	

exercise 3 Two important Indian tribes were the Cherokee and the Creek. Study the following chart. Then make sentences with *too* and *either*.

	Cherokee	*Creek*
lived in the Southeast	yes	yes
lived in the West	no	no
had many leaders	yes	yes
could write	no	no
were a large tribe	yes	yes
were hunters	yes	yes
had only one leader	no	no
were farmers	no	no
became traders	yes	yes
smoked tobacco	yes	yes
had alcoholic drinks	no	no
are rich now	no	no

1. The Cherokee lived in the Southeast, and the Creek did too.
2. The Cherokee didn't live in the West, and the Creek didn't either.
3. ______
4. ______
5. ______
6. ______
7. ______
8. ______
9. ______
10. ______
11. ______
12. ______

exercise 4 How many things do the students in your class have in common? For each question on page 170, try to find two students who answer yes and two students who answer no. Ask them to write their names in the blanks.

	YES	NO
1. Were you born in Mexico?		
2. Are you married?		
3. Do you have children?		
4. Do you speak German?		
5. Did you have coffee this morning?		
6. Can you ski?		
7. Did you study English in your country?		
8. Are you working?		
9. Did you come to the U.S. last year?		
10. Do you have any brothers?		

Now use your chart to make sentences with *too* and *either*.

examples: **Elena was born in Mexico, and Juana was too.**
Hans wasn't born in Mexico, and Heather wasn't either.

exercise 5 Complete this reading. Use the past tense of the verbs in parentheses.

The first Indians ___walked___ (walk) to America from Asia. Thousands of years _____(1)_____ (go) by. The Indians _____(2)_____ (go)

everywhere in America. Some Indian groups or tribes ______________ (hunt)
3

land and sea animals for food. Other tribes ______________ (learn) how to
4

farm. Several tribes ______________ (trade) food, clothing, salt, and gold.
5

Indians ______________ (be) part of nature. Their religion
6

______________ (have) gods from the sun, the moon, the rivers, and the
7

oceans. They ______________ (love) nature. Sometimes there
8

______________ (be) problems with other Indian tribes, but in general, the
9

Indians ______________ (do) well for thousands of years. Then, in 1492,
10

Columbus ______________ (come).
11

In the next four hundred years, millions of people ______________
12

(arrive) in America. This ______________ (be) a disaster for the Indians. The
13

new immigrants ______________ (push) the Indians farther and farther west.
14

Eventually the immigrants ______________ (force) the Indians to live in
15

places nobody else ______________ (want). These areas often
16

______________ (be) too dry or too cold to grow food or to hunt. These places
17

______________ (be) called reservations. Many Indians still live on reserva-
18

tions today.

Using What You've Learned

activity 1

Talking About Native Cultures. We have learned about Indians in one part of America. Did your country have native people? Does it have native people today? In groups of three or four, talk about what has happened to native peoples in your country or around the world.

activity 2

Adding Information. The whole class sits in a circle. One student makes a statement, and someone else adds another sentence with *either* or *too*. Use the present or the past tense. You don't have to tell the truth. Use your imagination!

examples: A: **I have five brothers.**
B: **Jake does too.**
A: **I don't have any sisters.**
B: **Eve doesn't either.**

TOPIC **two**

Simple Past Tense— More Irregular Verbs; Tag Questions

Setting the Context

prereading questions

When did Columbus arrive in America? Did many immigrants come to America after Columbus?

The Europeans

A Columbus arrived in the New World in 1492. At first, only a few Europeans followed. For the next three hundred years, about 500,000 immigrants came to America. Then the numbers grew very quickly. From 1815 to 1915, over thirty-two million Europeans left their countries for the United States. They came so they could find a better life.

B These immigrants were from many different cultures. They spoke many different languages. Most of them brought almost no money. But they got off the boats, and they found jobs. The biggest groups were from Germany and Italy.

discussion questions

Circle T (True) or F (False).

1. T F Thirty-two million people left Europe for the U.S. in 1815.
2. T F They came so that they could learn English.
3. T F They spoke different languages.
4. T F They brought a lot of money.
5. T F They found jobs.

exercise 1

Give the past tense forms for the following irregular verbs. (For a complete list of irregular verbs, see pages 308–309.)

be was, were	eat ______
become ______	freeze ______
begin ______	go ______
come ______	have ______
do ______	have to ______

A. More Irregular Verbs

simple form	past tense form
bring	brought
find	found
get	got
grow	grew
grow up	grew up
have	had
know	knew
leave	left
speak	spoke

exercise 2 Use the past tense of the verbs in parentheses to complete these sentences.

1. Tony _didn't grow up_ (not grow up) in the U.S.
2. He __________________ (grow up) in Italy.
3. Tony __________________ (find) a job in the steel mill in his town.
4. He __________________ (not find) a very good job.
5. Tony __________________ (not get) married when he was twenty.
6. He __________________ (get) married when he was eighteen.
7. Tony __________________ (speak) Italian.
8. He __________________ (not speak) English.
9. Tony __________________ (leave) Italy.
10. He __________________ (not leave) Italy forever.
11. Tony __________________ (bring) his wife and children to the U.S.
12. He __________________ (not bring) his father to the U.S.

exercise 3 Complete these readings with past tense forms of the verbs in parentheses. Then answer the questions. Use complete sentences in your answers.

1. My name is Antonio Bertelli, but my friends call me Tony. I _grew up_ (grow up) in a small town in Italy. In 1918, I ______________ (1) (get) married to Nina. In 1920 we ______________ (2) (have) our first child, Rene. Then, in 1921, I ______________ (3) (leave) Italy. My wife and daughter ______________ (4) (stay) in Italy. I ______________ (5) (come) to the United States.

   a. Where did Tony grow up? _He grew up in a small town in Italy._
   b. When did Tony get married to Nina? ______________________________
   c. When did he leave Italy? ______________________________

2. I ______________ (1) (get) on the boat in Naples, Italy, on September 20, 1921. I ______________ (2) (bring) one bag of clothes and some food. I ______________ (3) (get) to the U.S. on October 5th. First we ______________ (4) (go) to Ellis Island, the immigration center. Two days later, I ______________ (5) (be) in the greatest city in the world, New York!

a. When did Tony get on the boat? ____________________

b. What did he bring? ____________________

c. When did Tony get to the U.S.? ____________________

d. When did he leave Ellis Island? ____________________

3. I _____1_____ (be) very excited but also scared. I _____2_____ (have) only a little money. I _____3_____ (speak) a few words of English and French. But I really only _____4_____ (speak) Italian. Jack, my brother, _____5_____ (be) already in the States. He _____6_____ (help) me a lot. Soon I _____7_____ (find) a place to live and a job.

a. Was Tony relaxed? ____________________

b. Did he have a lot of money? ____________________

c. Did he know English? ____________________

d. Which language did he speak? ____________________

4. I _____1_____ (begin) to work for a construction company. I _____2_____ (not know) much about construction, but I _____3_____ (work) hard. Most of the guys on the job _____4_____ (speak) Italian. They _____5_____ (help) me with the job and with English too.

a. What didn't Tony know? ____________________

b. Did most of the guys speak Italian? ____________________

c. What did they help Tony with? ____________________

5. I _____1_____ (go) back to Italy every year, but in 1926, I _____2_____ (go) to Italy one last time. This time I _____3_____ (bring) my wife and daughter back to New York. We _____4_____ (find) a house with two bedrooms. In the next four years my son, John, and my last child, Virginia, _____5_____ (be) born. All three of my children _____6_____ (grow up) in New York. We _____7_____ (speak) Italian at home, but the children _____8_____ (learn) English at school. Life _____9_____ (not be) easy. We _____10_____ (be) just happy to be together.

a. When did Tony bring his wife and children to America? ____________

b. Did they find an apartment? ____________

c. Did they speak English at home? ____________

CULTURE NOTE

For more than 50 years, Ellis Island was the most important U.S. immigration station. Most immigrants arriving on the East Coast first went to Ellis Island. Ellis Island closed in 1943. Today it is a National Historic Site.

B. Tag Questions

statement	statement + tag question	notes
Tony came from Italy.	Tony came from Italy, **didn't he?**	Sometimes you think something is true, but you're not sure. To make sure, use tag questions.
He has three children.	He has three children, **doesn't he?**	
He is very old now.	He's very old now, **isn't he?**	
Rene wasn't born here.	Rene wasn't born here, **was she?**	
She can't speak Italian.	She can't speak Italian, **can she?**	
She moved here.	She moved here, **didn't she?**	

exercise 4 Tony's oldest daughter is named Rene. She got married and moved to California. Robert, one of her sons, is asking her questions about their family. Add tag questions to finish these sentences.

1. You left Italy in 1926, ___didn't you___?
2. You were only six years old, ________________?
3. You spoke Italian at home, ________________?
4. You got married in 1941, ________________?
5. Uncle John is in Florida, ________________?
6. Aunt Virginia has five kids, ________________?
7. You remember some Italian, ________________?
8. I look like my grandfather, ________________?
9. You talked to Grandpa last night, ________________?
10. I can have the car tonight, ________________?

exercise 5 Robert continues to ask his mother questions. Make the following into tag questions.

1. Grandpa didn't speak any French, ___did he___?
2. Grandma wasn't happy in New York, ________________?
3. She didn't learn English well, ________________?
4. You didn't know your grandparents well, ________________?
5. You didn't go back to Italy for many years, ________________?
6. You weren't in college during the war, ________________?
7. You can't read and write Italian, ________________?
8. You don't see your brother and sister often, ________________?
9. I don't have to do the dishes tonight, ________________?
10. You aren't serious, ________________?

Using What You've Learned

activity 1 **Asking Your Partner.** Work with a partner. You may know your partner already, but check to make sure about some things. Ask your partner questions about his or her life. Ask at least six tag questions. Make three positive and three negative questions. Then change roles.

examples: **You are married, aren't you?**
You didn't grow up in Switzerland, did you?

activity 2 **Telling Stories.** This is a picture of an immigrant to the United States. Give this woman a name, and tell which country she came from. Then tell the story of this woman. Use the following verbs at least once: *be, bring, come, find, get, go, grow up, leave, and speak.* You may use any other verbs you want.

example: **This is Sabine. She grew up in Rumania. She came to the U.S. in . . .**

TOPIC three

Simple Past Tense—More Irregular Verbs; even though; used to

Setting the Context

prereading questions Look at the map on page 179. Between 1820 and 1990, where did most immigrants to the United States come from? Where did most immigrants come from in the 1970s and 1980s?

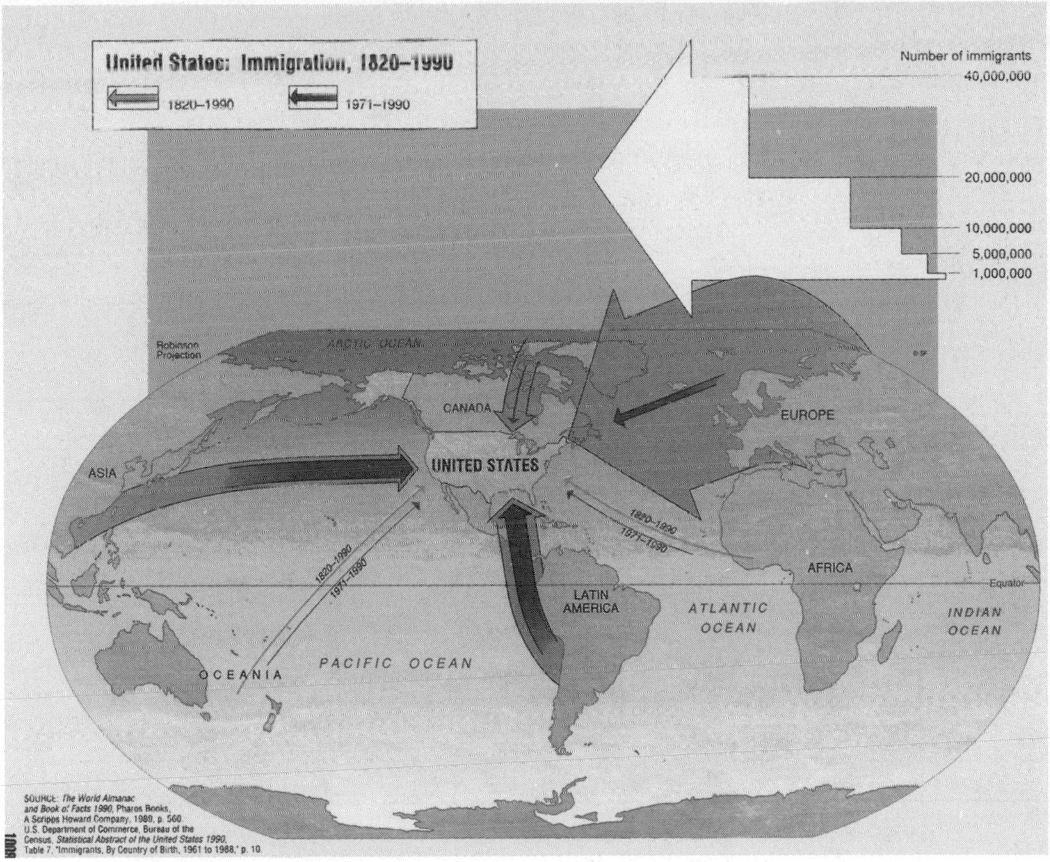

The Vietnamese

A Europeans used to be the largest group of immigrants to the United States. That began to change in the 1950s and 1960s. Today Asians and Latin Americans are the two largest groups of immigrants to the United States.

B Many of the Asians in the United States are from Vietnam. One of these Vietnamese immigrants is Dung Ha. He used to live in Saigon. After the war in Vietnam, there were many problems with the economy and the new government in Vietnam. Dung decided to leave even though it was very dangerous. Dung bought a place on a small boat. It cost a lot. He spent almost all his money. The boat went to Thailand. Dung spent two years in a refugee camp there. Then he came to the United States as a refugee. The U.S. government paid for his ticket to Los Angeles.

discussion questions

Circle T (True) or F (False). Correct the false sentences.

1. T F Europeans are the largest group of immigrants to the U.S.
2. T F Dung lived in Saigon.
3. T F It was safe to leave Vietnam.

4. T F Dung bought a small boat.
5. T F He spent most of his money.
6. T F Dung paid for his ticket to the U.S.

exercise 1 Fill in the past tense forms of these irregular verbs. If you can't remember, see pages 308–309.

be	was, were	freeze	
become		get	
begin		go	
bring		grow up	
come		have	
do		have to	
eat		know	
find		leave	
		speak	

A. *even though*

but	even though	notes
Dung was very tired, **but** he decided to stay up.	**Even though** he was very tired, he decided to stay up.	In many sentences, *even though* can be used instead of *but*. *Even though* comes at the beginning of these sentences. *But* comes in the middle.
He had a lot of work, **but** he couldn't stay awake.	**Even though** he had a lot of work, he couldn't stay awake.	

exercise 2 Omit *but* and use *even though* in these sentences.

example: California was very strange for Dung, but he liked it.

Even though California was very strange for Dung, he liked it.

1. Dung had relatives in Los Angeles, but he didn't know them well.
2. Dung liked L.A., but he wanted to live in a smaller city.
3. Dung's relatives wanted him to stay in L.A., but he moved to Santa Barbara.
4. His English was poor, but he got a job in a restaurant.
5. Dung worked hard in the restaurant, but he made very little money.
6. Dung couldn't speak English well, but he entered the community college and started studying electronics.
7. He was in school, but he continued to work in the restaurant.
8. The classes were difficult, but he did very well.

exercise 3 Match the sentences that contrast in the following list. Then make sentences with *even though*.

example: **Even though it is sunny, it is cold.**

1. It is sunny.	a. He left his family in Italy.
2. The Indians didn't have sailboats.	b. He can't find a girlfriend.
3. Tony came to the U.S.	c. It is cold.
4. Tony was in the U.S. for forty years.	d. He still goes to school.
5. Rene had four children.	e. He gets homesick sometimes.
6. Dung wants to get married.	f. The Indians were able to come to America.
7. Dung is working.	g. She really wanted to have six.
8. Dung enjoys the U.S. very much.	h. Tony never learned English very well.

exercise 4 Use your imagination to complete the following sentences.

example: Even though Dung gets homesick, he wants to stay in the U.S..

1. Even though it's cold outside, ______________________.
2. Even though it's a beautiful day, ______________________.
3. Even though Vern is rich, ______________________.
4. Even though Mark is poor, ______________________.
5. Even though John eats six meals a day, ______________________.
6. Even though Penny almost never eats, ______________________.

B. *Used to*

examples		notes
Dung **used to work** in the countryside.	(He doesn't work there now.)	*Used to* is followed by a simple verb. It means that something was true in the past but isn't true anymore.
There **used to be** a war in Vietnam.	(The war is over now.)	
He **used to have** two jobs.	(He has only one now.)	

exercise 5 When Dung is homesick, he thinks of all the things he used to do in Vietnam. Read each of the statements below. Then use your imagination to tell what Dung does now.

example: He used to live in Saigon.
Now he lives in California.

1. He used to eat rice every night.
2. He used to walk around Saigon.
3. He used to speak Vietnamese all day.
4. He used to play soccer.
5. He used to play all day.
6. He used to visit his uncles and aunts in Saigon.

exercise 6 Are you ever homesick? Do you miss things from your country? With a partner, make a list of at least ten things you used to do in your country—things you can't do now.

example: I used to see my friends every weekend. I can't do that anymore.

exercise 7 GROUP ACTIVITY

Which things are you the most homesick for? Sit in a circle with three or four other students. Tell *one* thing you *used to* do—the thing you miss the most from your country. Be sure to tell why you miss it so much.

More Irregular Verbs

simple form	past tense form	notes
buy cost pay spend	bought cost paid spent	These sentences have the same meaning: I *paid* $1,500 for a computer. I *spent* $1,500 for a computer. The computer *cost* $1,500.

activity 8

Complete these conversations. Use the past forms of the verbs *buy, cost, pay,* and *spend.* Add other information as needed.

1. DUNG: I just ___bought___ a new ___bicycle___!
   JIMMY: How much did it ___cost___?
   DUNG: It ___cost $125___.
2. ELEANA: I just ______________ a new ______________!
   JUAN: How much did you ______________?
   ELEANA: I ______________________________.
3. MARLYN: Lou just ______________ a new ______________!
   JOHN: How much did he ______________?
   MARILYN: He ______________________________.
4. ALFONSO: Martin just ______________ a new ______________!
   KATE: How much did it ______________?
   ALFONSO: He ______________________________.

activity 9

Complete this conversation between Dung and his friend Jimmy. Use the present or past tense of the verbs in parentheses.

DUNG: Hey, Jimmy! Guess what? I just ___bought___ (buy) a new tennis racket.

JIMMY: Wow! _____(1) (be) it expensive? How much _____(2) it _____(3) (cost)?

DUNG: It _____(4) (be) a great deal! It only _____(5) (cost) $150.

JIMMY: $150! That _____(6) (be) a lot of money. You _____(7) (not buy) anything else, _____(8) (do) you?

DUNG: Well, I _____(9) (get) a new camera yesterday.

JIMMY: But, you already __10__ (have) a camera. You __11__(buy) it last month. You __12__ (pay) $350 for it.

DUNG: Yes, but I really __13__ (need) a new one now. This new camera __14__ (do) many great things.

JIMMY: How much __15__ you __16__ (spend) on it?

DUNG: I __17__ (get) another great deal. This camera usually __18__ (cost) $500, but yesterday it __19__ (be) on sale. I only __20__ (pay) $450.

JIMMY: __21__ (be) you crazy? You __22__ (have to) pay rent for your apartment tomorrow. Where are you going to get enough money for rent?

DUNG: I __23__ (not be) sure, but . . . , Jimmy, __24__ you __25__ (want) to buy my old camera?

Using What You've Learned

activity

Making Conversations. With a partner, write at least six short conversations. (Look at the conversations in exercises 8 and 9.) Try to use the verbs *pay, cost,* and *spend* and other irregular verbs. Choose two of the conversations and, with your partner, perform them for the class.

TOPIC four

Simple Past Tense— More Irregular Verbs; Reported Speech and Related Structures

Setting the Context

prereading questions

What are some reasons why many people try to enter the United States illegally?

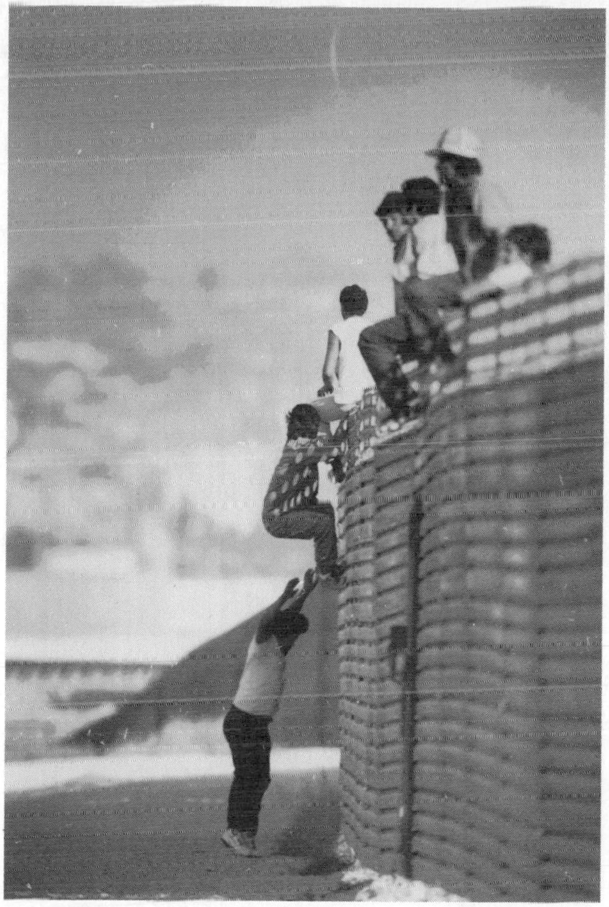

El Norte

A Juan was born in 1971 in a village near Oaxaca, Mexico. His village was in the mountains. It was in a beautiful area, but it was also very poor. Much of the time there was not enough food, water, or medicine.

B When Juan was a teenager, he heard that life was better in the United States. People said that you could get rich there. There used to be many young men in his village, but most of them left. Juan knew that they were in the United States.

CULTURE NOTE

Because of economic conditions, thousands of people try to enter the U.S. and Canada every year. Some villages and towns in Mexico have almost no young men. They are all working outside the country.

discussion questions

Circle T (True) or F (False). Correct the false sentences.

1. T F Juan lived in a poor village.
2. T F He heard that life was better in Mexico City.
3. T F People said he could learn English in the U.S.
4. T F There used to be a lot of young men in his village.
5. T F Juan knew that the young men were in Europe.

exercise 1

Give the past tense forms of these irregular verbs. If you can't remember, check pages 308–309.

be ___was, were___	freeze ______
become ______	get ______
begin ______	go ______
buy ______	grow up ______
bring ______	have ______
come ______	have to ______
cost ______	know ______
do ______	leave ______
eat ______	pay ______
find ______	speak ______
	spend ______

A. More Irregular Verbs

simple form	past tense form
hear	heard
know	knew
say	said

exercise 2 Complete these sentences. Use the past forms of the verbs in parentheses.

1. I heard (hear) many things about Mexico last night.
2. I _____ (not hear) many things about Guatemala last night.
3. I _____ (not know) that you were from Mexico.
4. I _____ (know) that you spoke Spanish.
5. Francisco _____ (say) that I could come to the meeting.
6. He _____ (not say) that I had to come.

B. Reported Speech and Related Structures: *hear, know,* and *say*

When we talk about what someone else said, we often use the verbs *said* and *heard.* This is called reported speech.

statement	reported speech	notes
"It is easy to enter the U.S."	He **said**[1] that it **was**[2] easy to enter the U.S.	The first verb is in the past, so the second verb is also in the past.
"The U.S. needs workers."	Juan **heard**[1] that the U.S. **needed**[2] workers.	The first verb is in the past, so the second verb is also in the past.

exercise 3 Juan heard a lot of things about the U.S. Change the statements into reported speech.

1. "Life is easy in the U.S."
   He heard that life was easy in the U.S.
2. "Life is hard in his village."
   Juan knew that ______________________
3. "It isn't difficult to enter the U.S."
   People said that ______________________
4. "Everyone in the U.S. is rich."
   People said that ______________________

5. "Jobs are easy to find."

People said that ______________________________

6. "All Americans live in nice houses."

Juan heard that ______________________________

7. "Many Mexicans become rich in the U.S."

People said that ______________________________

8. "They get good salaries."

Juan heard that ______________________________

9. "Americans don't worry about money."

He heard that ______________________________

10. "You can make a lot of money in the U.S."

People said that ______________________________

exercise 4

When did you come to the United States? What did you hear about the U.S. before you came? With a partner, list some things you heard. Then change them to reported speech. Use *I heard that, I knew that,* or *people said that.*

example: **There are many good jobs in the U.S.**

I heard that there were many good jobs in the U.S.

1. ______________________________
2. ______________________________
3. ______________________________
4. ______________________________
5. ______________________________

Which of the above ideas were true? Which were not?

C. More Irregular Verbs

simple form	past tense form
give	gave
lend	lent
see	saw

exercise 5 Complete the sentences with the past tense forms of the verbs.

1. I __gave__ (give) him five dollars.
2. I _________ (not give) him fifty dollars.
3. Miguel _________ (not lend) me his car.
4. He _________ (lend) me his bicycle.
5. Juan _________ (see) the border.
6. He _________ (not see) the police officer.

exercise 6 Complete the reading with the past tense forms of the verbs in parentheses.

In 1987, Juan __married__ (marry) Josefina. Later that year, they _____[1] (have) a baby girl. In 1989, Josefina's father _____[2] (lend) them some money. With this money, Juan _____[3] (buy) a bus ticket to Tijuana. A friend _____[4] (give) him the address of a man in Tijuana. This man _____[5] (be) a "coyote."* He _____[6] (can) take Juan across the border.

One morning in June, Juan _____[7] (say) good-bye to his wife and daughter. Like millions of Mexicans, he _____[8] (be) on his way to the United States.

Juan _____[9] (be) on the bus for more than three days. Finally, he _____[10] (arrive) in Tijuana. Juan _____[11] (be) hungry and tired. He _____[12] (buy) some food in the central marketplace. Then he _____[13] (go) to the house of the coyote. The coyote's name _____[14] (be) Pablo. Pablo _____[15] (say) that the price to go to the U.S. _____[16] (be) $500. Juan _____[17] (know) that $500 _____[18] (be) too high. Finally, they _____[19] (agree) on $300. Juan _____[20] (give) Pablo $150. He _____[21] (pay) the rest that night.

They _____[22] (leave) Pablo's house at 10:00 P.M. They _____[23] (go) outside of Tijuana. The place _____[24] (be) very dark, but Juan _____[25] (see) a fence. On the other side of the fence, Juan _____[26] (can) see a road and cars. Juan _____[27] (crawl) under the fence. He _____[28] (be) in the U.S.!

In the darkness, Juan _____[29] (see) a man. The man _____[30] (walk) toward him . . .

---

*coyote someone who helps people illegally enter the U.S. from Mexico

Using What You've Learned

activity

Writing a Story. Who was the man that Juan saw? What happened to Juan? What was life like for him in the U.S.? With a partner, finish Juan's story. Use some of the verbs in this chapter. Use any other verbs that you want. Your story should have at least fifteen sentences. When you are finished, share your story with the rest of the class.

CULTURE NOTE

Coyotes make money by helping people illegally cross the border into the U.S. They often charge hundreds of dollars to do this. They also sometimes take people's money but don't really help them.

checking your progress

Check your progress with structures from Chapters Five and Six. Be sure to review any problem areas.

Part 1: Choose the correct word(s) to complete each sentence.

1. I didn't finish, and she _____.
   a. did too
   b. didn't either
   c. didn't too
   d. either
2. Tony came from Italy, _____
   a. doesn't he?
   b. did he?
   c. came he?
   d. didn't he?
3. Even though Jinji has a car, _____
   a. she studies English at school.
   b. she takes the bus to school.
   c. she goes to school.
   d. she drives to school.
4. Who _____ in that house?
   a. used to live
   b. used to living
   c. living
   d. did lived
5. Juan heard that life _____ easy in the U.S.
   a. were
   b. will be
   c. is
   d. was
6. The water in the lakes _____ last year.
   a. freezed
   b. frozen
   c. froze
   d. didn't froze

7. Penny _____ German to the students.
   a. speak
   b. spoke
   c. did spoke
   d. speaked

8. I _____ $2,000 for the computer.
   a. cost
   b. bought
   c. payed
   d. spent

9. Mark _____ me $5,000.
   a. gave
   b. gived
   c. didn't gived
   d. will gives

10. I _____ that you were leaving.
   a. heard
   b. was heard
   c. hears
   d. heared

Part 2: Circle the correct words to complete this story. Circle "X" to show that nothing is necessary.

Juan (has / had)[1] a very difficult decision to make. Should he (goes / go)[2] to the U.S. or (stay / staying)[3] in Mexico with his family? He finally decided to (leaved / leave)[4]. The main reason was money. He heard that he (can / could)[5] make much more money in the U.S. than he could in Mexico.

One morning Juan (sayed / said)[6] goodbye to his wife and child and (got / gets)[7] on a bus to Tijuana. He didn't want to go, and his family didn't want him to go (too / either)[8]. (Eventhough / Even though)[9] he was sad, he was also excited. He (knew / knowed)[10] that he was about to start a new life.

CHAPTER seven

Work and Lifestyles

in this chapter

The Past Continuous Tense and Related Structures

Topic One: Affirmative Statements
Topic Two: Negative Statements and Questions
Topic Three: *While;* Contrast of Simple Past and Past Continuous Tenses
Topic Four: *When;* Contrast of Simple Past and Past Continuous Tenses

TOPIC **one**

Past Continuous Tense—Affirmative Statements

Setting the Context

prereading questions

What was the woman in the pictures doing five years ago? What is she doing now?

Five years ago

Now

Then and Now

A Five years ago, Monique was living with some relatives in a small apartment in Miami. They were all working then. Together, they paid the bills for the rent, telephone, and electricity. Monique was working as a dishwasher in the kitchen of Mercy Hospital. It was a hard job, but she liked the hospital. She was also attending English classes. She was learning a lot of new things. She was always busy and tired then. But she was happy, and she was excited about her future.

B Now Monique is working as a nurse's assistant at Mercy Hospital. Sometimes she visits the kitchen. She remembers when she was washing dishes there. Monique continues to think about her future.

discussion questions

1. When did Monique come to Miami?
2. What was Monique's first job? Where was it?
3. Where is she working now?

In the United States, it is common for people to change jobs. Do people in your country usually have one job for life? How often do people change jobs? Why?

A. Affirmative Statements

Subject + *was* or *were* + verb + *-ing*

singular	plural	notes
I **was working.** You **were working.** He / She / It } **was working.**	We / You / They } **were working.**	Use the past continuous tense to talk about past activities in progress at specific times such as *a minute ago, yesterday, last week, last month,* or *last year.*

exercise 1 Underline all the past continuous verbs in the reading on page 194.

exercise 2 Change the present continuous tense to the past continuous tense in these sentences. Change *now* to *five years ago.*

example: Monique is working at Mercy Hospital now.

Monique was working at Mercy Hospital five years ago.

1. She's living in a small apartment in Miami now.
2. Her relatives are all working and paying the bills together now.
3. She's improving her life now.
4. Now she's learning a lot of new things.
5. Now she's thinking about her future.

exercise 3 Change the sentences on page 196 to the past continuous tense. Add one of the time expressions to each sentence. Use each time expression at least once.

example: Monique is studying English now.

Monique was studying English five years ago.

TIME EXPRESSIONS:			
five years ago	*yesterday*	*last week*	*last year*

1. Monique is living in Miami now.
2. Monique's relatives are living together this year.
3. Our class is studying Chapter Seven now.
4. We're speaking English now.
5. I'm living in _____ (your city) now.

exercise 4 Meet Monique's neighbors. Complete these sentences. Use the past continuous tense of the verbs in parentheses.

1. My name is Sam. I used to be a plumber, but last year I lost my job. I was living (live) in Pittsburgh, and I ______(1)______ (work) at Pittsburgh Plumbing. I ______(2)______ (plan) to work until my retirement. Now I'm living in Miami, and I'm working for my cousin's company.
2. Hi. I'm Ana. I used to be a teacher, but I wanted to be an actress. Last year I ______(1)______ (live) in Hollywood. I ______(2)______ (try) to get a job in the movies. I ______(3)______ (dream) about my first movie. Now I'm a waitress. But you know what? I like it!
3. Hello. My name is Fred. I wanted my son to go to college, and he did go. After college, my son ______(1)______ (study) computers, and he ______(2)______ (invent) lots of crazy things. Big companies ______(3)______ (call) him. They ______(4)______ (try) to buy some of his inventions. I ______(5)______ (take) the phone messages. Now he's working in a car wash. What happened?

exercise 5 Use your own words and ideas to complete these sentences. Write about yourself.

example: Last year at this time, I was working in a bank.

1. A minute ago, I ______________________________.
2. At this time yesterday, I ______________________________.
3. At this time last Saturday, I ______________________________.
4. At this time last week, I ______________________________.
5. At this time last month, I ______________________________.

B. Contrast of Past and Present Continuous Tenses

	examples	notes
Present Continuous Tense	We**'re studying** Chapter Seven now.	Use the present continuous tense for action happening now.
Past Continuous Tense	We **were studying** Chapter Six last week.	Use the past continuous tense for action in progress in the past.

exercise 6 Meet some of the business people in Monique's neighborhood. Complete these readings. Use the past continuous or present continuous tense of the verbs in parentheses.

1. Last year at this time, I __was looking__ (look) for a job. I ______ (1) (read) the want ads in the newspaper, and I ______ (2) (send) resumes everywhere. I ______ (3) (become/also) very poor! Finally, I got a job. Today I ______ (4) (work) at Software Systems. I ______ (5) (write) computer programs, and I ______ (6) (help) with some special projects. I'm very happy, and I'm not poor anymore.

2. A year ago, we ______ (7) (look) for jobs. We ______ (8) (apply) for positions everywhere. We ______ (9) (feel) very worried. Then we started our own business. Today we ______ (10) (run) our own design company. We ______ (11) (do) advertising for many small businesses here. We ______ (12) (think) about some new projects too. And we ______ (13) (hire) an assistant! We feel very lucky today.

Using What You've Learned

activity 1

Talking About Past Activities. Work in small groups. Tell what you were doing at the times in this chart. Write what other students tell you.

NAME	LAST NIGHT AT MIDNIGHT	LAST YEAR AT THIS TIME	LAST SATURDAY NIGHT	AFTER CLASS YESTERDAY
example: Joe	He was doing homework.	He was living with his family.	He was dancing.	He was studying in the library.

activity 2

Describing Yourself. Write a paragraph about yourself like the ones in Exercise 6. Use this incomplete paragraph as a model.

Last year at this time, I ____

____.

I ____.

Then ____.

____

____.

Today I ____.

____

____.

TOPIC **two**

Past Continuous Tense—Negative Statements; Questions

Setting the Context

prereading questions

Who are the people in the picture? What are they doing?

Success!

People at Mercy Hospital like Monique and admire her for her hard work. The editor of the *Mercy Hospital Newsletter* is interviewing Monique for a short article.

EDITOR: You went to nursing school at night, right? You were also working as a dishwasher, weren't you?

MONIQUE: No, I wasn't working as a dishwasher then. I was working in a small restaurant. I was a waitress.

EDITOR: How much money were you making?

MONIQUE: Not very much. I was surprised at first. The hourly pay for a waitress is very low—below minimum wage. A waitress earns more money from tips.

EDITOR: Were you getting good tips?

MONIQUE: At first, I wasn't getting good tips. Then after a few months, I started making more in tips. I enjoyed the job too! I like people. My customers were teaching me English on the job.

EDITOR: What are your plans for the future? Are you finished studying?

MONIQUE: No, not yet. But let's talk about my plans another time.

discussion questions

Circle T (True) or F (False). Correct the false sentences.

1. T F Monique was working as a dishwasher when she started nursing school.
2. T F She was making a lot of money when she started working.
3. T F Monique didn't enjoy her job as a waitress.

A. Negative Statements

Subject + *was* or *were* + *not* + *ing*

long form		contractions	
I	**was not working.**	I	**wasn't working.**
You	**were not working.**	You	**weren't working.**
He / She / It	**was not working.**	He / She / It	**wasn't working.**
We / You / They	**were not working.**	We / You / They	**weren't working.**

exercise 1

Change these statements to negative sentences. Use contractions.

example: Monique was working as a dishwasher then.
Monique wasn't working as a dishwasher then.

1. Monique was earning a lot of money.
2. Monique was studying French.
3. At first, Monique was getting good tips.
4. Monique and her relatives were living in New York.
5. Our class was studying Chapter Nine last week.
6. We were speaking Chinese in class yesterday.

exercise 2

Jean Paul is Monique's brother. Read Jean Paul's story on page 201. Then rewrite his story and change all the underlined verbs to negative forms.

example: I was having a good time there.
I wasn't having a good time there.

Hi, I'm Jean Paul, Monique's youngest brother. I was living with Monique and other relatives in Miami. I was having a good time there. I was working in a grocery store. I was earning a lot of money. I was making friends. I was having a lot of fun. I was excited about the future.

B. Yes / No Questions and Short Answers

yes/no questions	short answers: Affirmative	short answers: Negative
Was I **working?**	Yes, you **were.**	No, you **weren't.**
Were you **working?**	Yes, I **was.**	No, I **wasn't.**
Was {he / she / it} **working?**	Yes, {he / she / it} **was.**	No, {he / she / it} **wasn't.**
Were {you / we / they} **working?**	Yes, {we / they} **were.**	No, {we / they} **weren't.**

exercise 3 Write the questions for these statements.

1. *Were you living here last month?*

   Yes, I was living here last month.

2. ____________________

   No, Monique wasn't making a lot of money.

3. ____________________

   No, Jean Paul wasn't having fun.

4. ____________________

   Yes, Monique's relatives were all working hard.

5. ____________________

   Yes, Monique's relatives were living in Miami.

6. ______________________________

Yes, I was studying hard last night.

7. ______________________________

No, I wasn't speaking my native language in English class!

exercise 4 Answer these questions. Write short answers.

example: Were you visiting Las Vegas last week?

No, I wasn't.

1. Were your classmates working last night?

____

2. Was your teacher working hard last week?

____

3. Were you living in Vancouver last year?

____

4. Were you going to school before you came here?

____

5. Were you earning a lot of money in your last job?

____

6. Were you sleeping at midnight last night?

____

C. Information Questions

Question word + was / were + subject + verb + *ing* + time expression

questions	possible answers
What was he **doing** yesterday?	He was working.
Where were we **meeting** last year?	We were meeting in San Francisco.
When was it **arriving?**	It was arriving at 3:00.
Why were you **taking** a course last month?	Because I had to.
How was she **doing**?	She was doing well.
How much was he **earning**?	He was earning a lot of money.

questions	possible answers
Who* + *was* + verb + *-ing	
Who was doing that job?	John was doing it.
Who was calling all last night.	David was.

exercise 5

Use these question words to complete the sentences below. More than one word can be used in some sentences.

Who *What* *When* *Where* *Why* *How* *How much*

1. ___What___ were you doing at 10:00 last night?
2. __________ were you saying a minute ago?
3. __________ was helping you with the assignment?
4. __________ was he going?
5. __________ were you getting to work?
6. __________ were you working there?
7. __________ were they earning money?
8. __________ was he running out the door?
9. __________ was coming in the door?
10. __________ were you earning last year?

Using What You've Learned

activity 1

Learning About Another Student. Write ten true or false statements about things you were doing in the past. The sentences can be affirmative or negative.

1. ______________________________
2. ______________________________
3. ______________________________
4. ______________________________
5. ______________________________
6. ______________________________
7. ______________________________
8. ______________________________

9. ______________________________

10. ______________________________

When you finish, work with a partner. Take turns reading your statements to each other. Decide which of your partner's sentences are true and which are false. Your partner will do the same for your sentences. Finally, tell each other the truth.

example: A: **Last year I was living in Texas.**
B: **False. I think you were living in your home country.**
A: **You're right. I was living in Laos last year.**

activity 2

Information Gap. Here is more information about Monique and Jean Paul. Work with a partner. Don't look at your partner's chart. Ask information questions to complete your chart.

STUDENT A				
Name	10 Years Ago / Living	Last Year / Dating	Last Year / Earning	Now / Earning
Monique	________	Mike	________	$1,500
Jean Paul	Haiti	________	$800 a month	________

STUDENT B				
Name	10 Years Ago / Living	Last Year / Dating	Last Year / Earning	Now / Earning
Monique	Haiti	________	$1,000 a month	________
Jean Paul	________	nobody	________	$1,000

activity 3 **Writing a Newsletter Article.** Interview a partner. Write ten interview questions to ask your partner. Use the past continuous tense. Then ask your partner the questions. Take notes on your partner's answers.

	QUESTIONS	NOTES
example:	Where were you living five years ago?	In Argentina.
1.		
2.		
3.		
4.		
5.		
6.		
7.		
8.		
9.		
10.		

Finally, on your own paper, write a newsletter article about your partner. Use your interview notes.

TOPIC three

While; Contrast of Simple Past and Past Continuous Tenses

Setting the Context

prereading questions Look at the picture on page 206. What is the man on the bicycle doing?

Riding the Streets of Manhattan

A While Monique was becoming successful in Miami, Jean Paul was having a hard time. He wasn't earning much money, and he wasn't making new friends. He decided to leave Miami. His favorite cousin was living in New York, so Jean Paul moved to New York.

B Jean Paul got a job at a delivery company. He was delivering mail by bicycle to offices in Manhattan. He loved his job. While he was earning money, he was having fun. He had many adventures while he was working.

C One day while Jean Paul was riding across the city, he saw an old friend. It was his old girlfriend from Haiti! She was waiting to cross the street. Imagine that! Life was getting better and better for Jean Paul.

discussion questions

Answer the following questions.

1. Was Jean Paul successful in Miami?
2. Where was his cousin living?
3. What was Jean Paul's job in New York?
4. Who did he see while he was riding down the street?

CULTURE NOTE

In many big cities, cars are not the best kind of transportation. They cause traffic and pollution. What kinds of transportation are best in the big cities in your country? Why?

A. While

examples

***While* + past continuous tense, + past continuous tense**

While Monique **was becoming** successful, Jean Paul **was having** a hard time.

While she **was working** in an office, he **was** still **looking** for a job.

Past continuous tense + *while* + past continuous tense

Monique **was becoming** successful **while** Jean Paul **was having** a hard time.

She **was working** in an office **while** he **was** still **looking** for a job.

notes

While is often used to connect two actions in the past that were happening at the same time.

Use a comma only when *while* is at the beginning of the sentence.

exercise 1 Circle all the uses of *while* in Jean Paul's story on page 206. Underline all the verbs in those sentences. Tell what tense each verb is.

exercise 2 Complete these sentences with the correct pronouns.

1. While Monique was living in Haiti, ___she___ was selling fish.
2. While Monique was living in Miami, _________ was studying English.
3. While Monique's relatives were living together, _________ were paying all the bills together.
4. While Jean Paul was living in Miami, _________ wasn't making friends.
5. Jean Paul was having a good time while _________ was working.

exercise 3 Combine these pairs of sentences with *while*. If the subject of both sentences is the same, use a pronoun.

example: Monique was studying nursing. Monique was working as a waitress.

While Monique was studying nursing, she was working as a waitress.

1. Jean Paul was working in New York. Jean Paul wasn't studying.
2. Monique was working at the hospital. Monique was saving money.
3. Jean Paul was living in New York. Monique was living in Miami.
4. Monique was making friends in Miami. Jean Paul was making friends in New York.
5. We were studying Chapter Three. We were talking about friends and families.

B. Past Continuous Tense Versus Simple Past Tense in Sentences with *while*

Use *while* with the past continuous tense to show the longer action. Use the simple past tense for the action that interrupts or stops the longer action. Use a comma only when *while* is at the beginning of the sentence.

***While* + past continuous tense, + simple past tense**	**Simple past tense + *while* + past continuous tense**
While Jean Paul **was riding** his bicycle, he **saw** an old friend.	Jean Paul **saw** an old friend **while** he **was riding** his bicycle.
While Monique **was doing** the dishes, she **had** a good idea.	Monique **had** a good idea **while** she **was doing** the dishes.

exercise 4 Complete each sentence with the simple past tense or the past continuous tense of the verb in parentheses.

1. While Jean Paul was working, he ___had___ (have) many adventures.
2. While Jean Paul was riding down Fifth Avenue, he __________ (see) an accident.
3. While Jean Paul was going up to the 66th floor on an elevator, the electricity __________ (go) out.
4. While Jean Paul __________ (cross) 42nd Street, he almost ran into an old man.
5. While Jean Paul __________ (make) a delivery at the Empire State Building, he saw an accident.
6. While Jean Paul was resting in front of the World Trade Center, a man suddenly __________ (take) a woman's purse and __________ (run) away.

exercise 5 Join the following pairs of sentences. Use *while*.

example: Jean Paul was looking around. Jean Paul had an accident.
While Jean Paul was looking around, he had an accident.

1. Monique was working. Monique got a phone call from Jean Paul.
2. Jean Paul was talking. Monique was crying.
3. Jean Paul was telling about the accident. Monique was writing notes.
4. Jean Paul and Monique were talking. The operator asked for more money.
5. Jean Paul was saying good-bye. Jean Paul said he was OK.

Using What You've Learned

activity 1 **Information Gap.** Jean Paul and Monique have different schedules. Work with a partner. Look at one of the two charts on page 210. Don't look at your partner's chart. Ask your partner what Jean Paul or Monique was doing at a particular time yesterday. Write down the information

example: A: **What was Monique doing at 7:00 yesterday morning?**
B: **She was sleeping.**

STUDENT A

Jean Paul's Schedule		*Monique's Schedule*	
7:00 A.M.	go to work	7:00 A.M.	*She was sleeping.*
7:30	make 1st delivery	7:30	______
10:00	take a break	10:00	______
12:00 (noon)	eat lunch	12:00 (noon)	______
5:00 P.M.	make last delivery	5:00 P.M.	______
6:00	go home	6:00	______
7:00	eat dinner	7:00	______
10:00	watch a movie with his girlfriend	10:00	______

STUDENT B

Monique's Schedule		*Jean Paul's Schedule*	
7:00 A.M.	sleep	7:00 A.M.	*He was going to work.*
7:30	sleep	7:30	______
10:00	get up	10:00	______
12:00 (noon)	study	12:00 (noon)	______
5:00 P.M.	go to work	5:00 P.M.	______
6:00	start work	6:00	______
7:00	work	7:00	______
10:00	take a break	10:00	______

activity 2

Comparing Past Activities. Work with a partner. Talk about what you and your partner were doing at this time last year. Write one sentence on the board. Discuss your sentence with the class.

example: *While Carlos was studying in high school, Mila was taking care of her baby.*

activity 3 **Writing a Story** Finish this story about Jean Paul. Add at least five sentences.

While Jean Paul was waiting for a light, he saw his old girlfriend from Haiti. Her name was ______________ . While they were talking, he wrote down her telephone number. Then ______________________________

____

____

____

When you finish, work with a partner. Read each other's stories. Which story do you like best?

TOPIC four

When; *Contrast of Simple Past and Past Continuous Tenses*

Setting the Context

prereading questions

Where is the man in the picture?
What is in his hand?

My Own Business

A I remember that moment so well. It was one of the happiest moments in my life. Oh, excuse me. I should introduce myself first. My name is Al. I'm a mechanic at a Golf service station.

B Two weeks ago I got a letter from my father. It had the words I was waiting to read. My brother is finally going to come to the United States! And he's coming with a lot of money. We can open our own business! What was I doing when the letter arrived? Well, I was fixing Mr. Wilson's Mercedes. I was starting up the engine. I turned off the engine when I saw the letter from my father. My hands were shaking when I picked up the letter. My heart was beating fast when I opened the envelope.

C Think of it—Rismani's Service Station. Doesn't that sound beautiful?

discussion questions

1. Who is Al?
2. Where does he work?
3. What did he get from his father?
4. How did he feel when he read the letter?

A. *When*

examples	notes
***When* + simple past tense + past continuous tense** **When** the phone **rang,** I **was talking** to my brother. **When** I **saw** the fire, I **was walking** to work.	Use *when* with the simple past tense for the action that stops or interrupts the longer action. Use the past continuous tense with the longer action.
***When* + simple past tense + simple past tense** **When** the phone **rang,** I **answered** it. **When** I **saw** the fire, I **called** for help.	Sometimes both actions are short. In this case, use *when* with the first action. Use the simple past tense with both actions.

exercise 1

Circle all the uses of *when* in the reading on page 211 and 212. Underline all the verbs in those sentences. Tell what tense each verb is.

exercise 2

Complete these sentences with *when* or *while.*

example: ___While___ Al was working at the Golf station, he saved a lot of money.

1. ______________ Al was fixing a Mercedes, the letter arrived.
2. ______________ Al's brother arrived at the airport, Al was waiting for him.
3. ______________ the Rismani brothers found a good gas station, they bought it.
4. ______________ the Rismani brothers opened their gas station, they weren't making much money.

5. ______________ the Rismani brothers were waiting for more customers, they were working hard.

6. ______________ the business improved, the Rismanis hired an assistant.

exercise 3 Join each pair of sentences. Use *when*.

example: The new highway opened. The Rismanis were ready for more customers.

When the new highway opened, the Rismanis were ready for more customers.

1. Rismani's Service Station became successful. The brothers bought a second service station.
2. Al's daughter entered college. Al was working seven days a week.
3. Al's daughter graduated from college. Al was working six days a week.
4. The Rismanis bought another service station. Al's daughter became a manager.
5. Al's son entered college. Al was working five days a week.

exercise 4 Complete these sentences. Use the simple past or the past continuous tense.

1. When I decided to come to the United States, I started to save money.
2. When I left my country, I ______________________________.
3. When I arrived in the United States, ______________________________.
4. When I first met my classmates, ______________________________.
5. While I was going home from school one day, ______________________________.
6. While our teacher was talking, ______________________________.
7. While the students were taking a test, ______________________________.

B. Simple Past Tense Versus Past Continuous Tense

examples	notes
Al **got up** every day at 6:00.	Use the simple past tense for past repeated action.
Al **went** to bed at 10:00.	Use the simple past tense for a short action at a time in the past.
Al **was sleeping** at 11:00.	Use the past continuous tense for an action in progress in the past.

exercise 5 Circle the correct verbs in these sentences.

example: Al (ate / was eating) breakfast quickly at 6:00 every morning.

1. Monique (went / was going) to bed at 10:00 at night in Haiti.
2. Monique (slept / was sleeping) at 6:00 in the morning.
3. Jean Paul (worked / was working) every day for eight hours in Miami.
4. Jean Paul (worked / was working) at 8:00 yesterday morning.
5. Al (fixed / was fixing) Mr. Wilson's car when the letter arrived.
6. Al (fixed / was fixing) Mr. Wilson's car last week.

exercise 6 Remember, some verbs are never used in continuous tenses. (See page 94.) Complete these readings with the correct forms of the verbs in parentheses. Use the past continuous tense when possible.

Al and his brother bought their own business in 1989. Al was working hard, but he ____knew____ (know) that it ______(1) (be) necessary. He ______(2) (work) twelve hours a day, but he ______(3) (understand) he had to. He ______(4) (like) the location because it ______(5) (be) near a large highway. Day by day, they ______(6) (get) more and more business.

exercise 7 Complete these readings with the correct form of the verbs in parentheses. Use these tenses: simple present, present continuous, simple past, or past continuous.

1. When Monique ____arrived____ (arrive) from Haiti, she ______(1) (dream) of a good future. When she ______(2) (see) Miami for the first time, she ______(3) (love) it. While she ______(4) (make) her dreams come true, she ______(5) (work) hard. Now, ten years later, Monique ______(6) (be) a nursing supervisor. She ______(7) (live) with two young cousins from Haiti. They ______(8) (arrive) last year with dreams of a good future. Monique ______(9) (help) them.

2. While Jean Paul ______1______ (live) in Miami, he ______2______ (not be) happy. When he ______3______ (decide) to move to New York, he ______4______ (feel) sad.

Now, ten years later, Jean Paul's life ______5______ (be) much better. He ______6______ (own) his own company, J.P.'s Speedy Delivery. He ______7______ (earn) a lot of money, and he ______8______ (not work) many hours. Jean Paul is married. He ______9______ (have) three children.

3. While Al ______1______ (work) at the Golf station, he ______2______ (save) his money. He ______3______ (work) twelve hours a day when he ______4______ (buy) his second service station.

Now, ten years later, Al ______5______ (not work). He and his brother ______6______ (own) five Rismani service stations. They ______7______ (live) in Miami, and their children ______8______ (manage) the service stations.

Using What You've Learned

activity

Talking About People. Work with a partner. Choose one of the two people. Take turns and tell a story about him or her. Give the person a name. Tell about the person's life five years ago. Then tell about his or her life now.

GROUP ACTIVITY

When you finish, join another pair of students. Tell one another about the people. Compare your stories.

CHAPTER eight

Food and Nutrition

in this chapter

Count Nouns and Noncount Nouns

Topic One: Count Nouns; *a, an, some* and *any*; Questions with *how many*

Topic Two: Noncount Nouns; *some* and *any*

Topic Three: Counting Units and Units of Measurement: Questions with *how much*; *how much* Versus *how many*

Topic Four: Common Noncount Nouns; *a lot (of)*; *a little* Versus *a few*; *not much* Versus *not many*

TOPIC one
Count Nouns; a, an, some, and any; Questions with how many

Setting the Context

prereading questions Where are these people? What is the older man doing? What information does the young man want?

What Do Americans Eat?

A Some people say that North Americans don't eat healthy food. What *do* Americans eat? There are some easy ways to find out. For example, is there a supermarket near your home? Go and take a look—at the shoppers, at the shelves, and at the shopping carts. What are people buying?

B Don't stop yet. Are there any special food stores nearby? Are there oriental, vegetarian, or natural foods stores? Take a look at the shoppers and their shopping carts. How many people are shopping in the store? What are they buying?

C And finally, are there some takeout or fast-food restaurants in your neighborhood? Look at them at lunchtime or dinnertime. Are there many customers? What kinds of food are they ordering?

D Look around you, and you can begin to get an idea of how Americans spend money on food.

discussion questions

1. How can you find out about what people eat? Give some examples from the reading, and add your own ideas.
2. Do you think North Americans eat healthy food?
3. In your native country, do people shop in supermarkets, or do they go to many smaller stores?

CULTURE NOTE

North American supermarkets have many kinds of cold breakfast cereals. How many kinds of breakfast cereal can you find on the shelves of a supermarket in your country?

A. Count Nouns

A noun names a person, place, thing, idea, or emotion. There are two basic types of nouns—count nouns and noncount nouns. Count nouns are things you can count, such as chairs and people.

examples		notes
Singular	***Plural***	
box	**boxes**	Count nouns have singular and plural forms. (See Chapter One for spelling rules for *-s* endings.)
city	**cities**	
customer	**customers**	
shelf	**shelves**	

Common Irregular Count Nouns

examples		notes
Singular	***Plural***	
person	**people**	(See Chapter One for a more complete list of irregular noun plurals.)
child	**children**	
man	**men**	
woman	**women**	

exercise 1 Write the plurals of these count nouns.

1. person	people	**11.** church	__________
2. woman	__________	**12.** apple	__________
3. party	__________	**13.** mouse	__________
4. child	__________	**14.** loaf	__________
5. orange	__________	**15.** cherry	__________
6. box	__________	**16.** dish	__________
7. radio	__________	**17.** man	__________
8. baby	__________	**18.** tomato	__________
9. goose	__________	**19.** shelf	__________
10. wife	__________	**20.** foot	__________

B. *Some* and *any* with count nouns

	examples	notes
Question	Do you have **any** apples or oranges at home? Would you like **some** apples?	Use *some* or *any* in questions.
Affirmative Statement	I have **some** apples at home.	Use *some* in affirmative statements.
Negative Statement	I do**n't** have **any** oranges at home.	Use *any* in negative statements.

exercise 2 Imagine that you are Mark or Linda on page 221. Look at "your" kitchen, but not at your partner's. Ask questions about your partner's kitchen, using the ten cues on page 221. Use *any* in your questions.

examples:

apples
A: **Linda, do you have any apples?**
B: **Yes, I have some.**

potato chips
B: **Mark, do you have any potato chips?**
A: **No, I don't have any.**

1. grapes
2. frozen dinners
3. oranges
4. potatoes
5. onions
6. bananas
7. canned tomatoes
8. carrots
9. peas
10. apples

C. Questions with *how many*

How many **+ count noun + auxiliary verb + subject + verb**

questions	possible answers	notes
How many bananas do you have?	I have three.	Use *how many* in questions with count nouns.
How many eggs do you need for the cake?	I need two.	

exercise 3

What do you eat each week? What do you drink? Work in small groups. Take turns asking and answering questions with *how many* and the fifteen word cues below.

example: bananas

A: **How many bananas do you eat each week?**
B: **I eat a banana almost every day.**
C: **I eat about two bananas a week.**
D: **I don't eat any bananas. I don't like them.**

1. eggs
2. apples
3. glasses of milk
4. cookies
5. avocados
6. salads
7. ice-cream cones
8. bags of potato chips
9. bottles of beer
10. cups of coffee
11. bowls of rice
12. oranges
13. hamburgers
14. cans of soda
15. sandwiches

D. *A* and *an* with singular count nouns

words beginning with consonant sounds	words beginning with vowel sounds	notes
a banana **a** house **a** European	**an** egg **an** hour **an** American	*A* or *an* means "one" or "any." Use *a* before a consonant sound and *an* before a vowel sound.

exercise 4

Use *a* or *an* before each of these nouns.

1. an apartment
2. a house
3. ______ egg
4. ______ banana
5. ______ orange
6. ______ apple
7. ______ hour
8. ______ European
9. ______ stove
10. ______ oven
11. ______ table
12. ______ knife

exercise 5 Complete this reading. Use *a* or *an* before singular nouns and *X* (no article) before plural nouns.

I'm Linda. Don't tell anybody, but I love fast food. I never make __a__ big breakfast. It takes too long. Instead I usually eat _____ (1) bowl of _____ (2) Chocoflakes. Occasionally I eat _____ (3) egg for breakfast on the weekends. For a snack, I sometimes have _____ (4) apple or _____ (5) orange, but I like junk food better. I love _____ (6) potato chips, _____ (7) corn chips, and _____ (8) pretzels. My favorite lunch is _____ (9) hot dog or _____ (10) hamburger, _____ (11) french fries, and _____ (12) big piece of chocolate cake. I don't cook lunch of course! I always buy _____ (13) lunches near work. My dinners are simple too. I usually have _____ (14) microwave dinner or _____ (15) can of spaghetti, _____ (16) can of diet soda, and _____ (17) ice-cream sundae. I really have _____ (18) terrible eating habits!

exercise 6 Complete this conversation with *a, an, some,* or *any.*

MARK: We should go grocery shopping. We need __some__ things for dinner. I want to make __an__ omelet and _____ (1) potatoes, but we don't have _____ (2) potatoes. I want to make _____ (3) apple pie too, but we don't have _____ (4) apples. We also need _____ (5) cleaning supplies.

THOMAS: You're right. There's _____ (6) broom, _____ (7) vacuum cleaner, and _____ (8) sponges here, but I don't see _____ (9) cleaning supplies. By the way, who is going to clean?

MARK: I'm cooking, so that means you're cleaning.

THOMAS: Hey, let's forget about shopping! I'd like _____ (10) hamburger. Let's go out for dinner, OK?

Using What You've Learned

activity 1 **Talking About Food.** What food and household items do you have in your home? Work with a partner. Ask questions with *any* about things in your own homes. Give true answers. Use the cues from exercise 2 on page 221 and the words below. You can also add your own words.

example: **Do you have any tomatoes in your home?**

1. tomatoes	**3.** sponges	**5.** frying pan
2. paper towels	**4.** knives	**6.** hot dogs

activity 2

GROUP ACTIVITY

Using a Questionnaire. Find out what people in your class or community really eat. Here's a questionnaire to help you. Ask three different people the questions. Add one question of your own. Then work in small groups and compare your answers.

HOW MANY DO YOU EAT OR DRINK EACH WEEK?	Age: _____ Sex: _____	Age: _____ Sex: _____	Age: _____ Sex: _____
1. How many cups of coffee or tea do you drink each week? 2. How many apples, oranges, or bananas do you eat? 3. How many salads do you eat? 4. How many sandwiches do you eat? What kind? 5. Do you eat any microwave meals? How many? 6. How many times a week do you eat in fast-food restaurants? 7. ______________________ ______________________			

TOPIC two

Noncount Nouns; some and any

Setting the Context

prereading questions

Many people do not eat certain types of food. Look at the pictures below and describe them. Do you eat or drink these things?

I Don't Want Any, Thank You

There are different ideas about what you should eat. There are also many ideas about what you should *not* eat! Some of these ideas come from religion. For example, Muslims don't eat any pork because of their religion. Many Jews don't eat any pork either. Some Christians don't eat meat on Fridays. Other Christians don't drink any wine or coffee. Many Buddhists never eat any meat or eggs at all. They eat a lot of rice, beans, fruit, and nuts instead.

discussion questions

1. Do Muslims eat pork?
2. Do some Jews eat pork?
3. What are some things Buddhists don't eat?
4. In your religion or culture, are there rules about certain types of food?

A. Noncount Nouns

Noncount nouns can be ideas *(freedom),* feelings *(love),* activities *(golf),* or things we measure *(oil)* or group together *(furniture).* Noncount nouns are always singular. Do not add *-s* to these nouns, and do not use *a* or *an* with them.

Noncount Nouns Versus Count Nouns—Names of Foods

Noncount Nouns			Count Nouns		
examples		**notes**	**singular**	**plural**	**notes**
bread	**flour**	People usually measure these items.	**apple**	**apples**	People usually count these items.
butter	**rice**		**banana**	**bananas**	
coffee	**tea**		**potato**	**potatoes**	

exercise 1

Write *C* in front of count nouns and *N* in front of noncount nouns.

1. __C__ apple
2. _____ tomato
3. _____ rice
4. _____ cheese
5. _____ banana
6. _____ meat
7. _____ egg
8. _____ juice
9. _____ milk
10. _____ potato
11. _____ sugar
12. _____ sandwich

B. *some* and *any* with Noncount nouns

	examples	notes
Question	Would you like **some** tea? Do you have **any** coffee at home?	Use *some* or *any* in questions.
Affirmative Statement	I have **some** Colombian coffee at home.	Use *some* in affirmative statements.
Negative Statement	I do**n't** have **any** tea at home.	Use *any* in negative statements.

exercise 2 Work with a partner. Choose a shopping list (Student A on this page or Student B on page 227). Make questions with *some* or *any.* Use the twelve words on page 227. Ask each other a question about each word. Write down your partner's answers, but do not look at your partner's list. Can you guess what meal your partner is shopping for?

STUDENT A

Shopping List

ice cream
lettuce
mustard
ketchup
milk
rice
coffee
meat

Shopping List

butter
tea
jam
cheese
sugar
milk
coffee
bread
cereal

example:	butter	butter
	A: **Do you need some butter?**	B: **Do you need any butter?**
	B: **Yes, I do.**	A: **No, I don't.**

1. rice	**5.** tea	**9.** cereal
2. milk	**6.** mustard	**10.** meat
3. coffee	**7.** jam	**11.** ice cream
4. sugar	**8.** ketchup	**12.** lettuce

exercise 3

You are having a party. Work in a chain. Ask and answer questions about the foods and drinks from the list below. Use *some* in your questions. Remember to make count nouns plural. Give true answers.

examples: soda pretzel

A: **Would you like some soda?**
B: **Yes, please.**
B: **Would you like some pretzels?**
C: **No, thanks.**

1. potato chip	**6.** juice	**11.** cookie
2. fresh vegetable	**7.** soda	**12.** fresh fruit
3. dip	**8.** coffee	**13.** grape
4. peanut	**9.** cream or sugar	**14.** watermelon
5. popcorn	**10.** cake	**15.** apple

Using What You've Learned

activity

Talking About Parties and Eating Habits. What do people in your country or culture serve at a formal party? At an informal get-together? At a birthday party? In a small group, take turns describing food at typical parties in your cultures. Use this chart to help you write your information.

Name				
Country				
Informal get-togethers				
Birthday parties				
Weddings				

TOPIC three

Counting Units and Units of Measurement; Questions with how much; how much *Versus* how many

Setting the Context

Who are these people? What are they cooking? Why are they cooking this?

World's largest omelet	1994	160,000 eggs (made by Swatch in Yokohama, Japan)
World's largest chocolate chip cookie	1992	measured 1,001 square feet more than 3 million chocolate chips (made at Santa Anita Fashion Park in California, USA)
World's largest lollipop	1994	weighed 3,011 pounds (made at Bon Bon in Holme Olstrup, Denmark)
World's largest loaf of bread	1991	measured 3,491 feet, 9 inches long (made at Hyatt Regency Hotel in Guadalajara, Mexico)

Guinness Book of World Records, Bantam Books, 1994

Too Much and Not Enough

A Many people like to read the *Guinness Book of World Records,* and some people want to be in it! How do people get their names in the book? They do something completely new and different, such as making the world's largest omelet with 160,000 eggs.

B For many people, it is fun to make world records. It is a challenge. But who ate the omelet?

C While some people are making world records, other people do not have much food to eat. Hunger is a very serious problem in the United States and around the world. How many elderly people do not have enough money to buy good food? How many children go to bed without dinner? Unfortunately, the answer is *too* many.

discussion questions

1. How many chocolate chips were in the world's largest chocolate chip cookie?
2. How much did the world's largest lollipop weigh?
3. Where was the largest loaf of bread made?
4. According to the reading, is hunger a problem in the United States?

CULTURE NOTE

Hunger is a problem in many countries. Many Americans don't have enough food to eat. Is hunger a problem in your country?

A. Common Counting Units

Counting units are used with many kinds of food and household items. *Of* follows all these expressions except *dozen.* In measurement and recipes, other units are also used, such as *yards* and tea*spoons.* (See page 232 for a chart of these.)

bag	flour, potatoes, potato chips, sugar, etc.
bar	candy, hand soap, etc.
bottle	detergent, ketchup, juice, soda, and other liquids
box	cereal, laundry detergent, etc.
bunch	bananas, carrots, grapes, green onions, flowers, etc.
can	soda, soup, vegetables, tuna, etc.
carton	eggs, ice cream, milk, etc.
dozen	eggs
gallon, quart, pint	all liquids, ice cream, yogurt
head	cabbage, cauliflower, lettuce
jar	jam, mayonnaise, mustard, peanut butter, etc.
loaf	bread
package	cookies, potato chips, spaghetti, etc.
piece	bread, cake, meat, cheese, etc.
pound, ounce	cheese, meat, poultry, fruits, vegetables, etc.
roll	paper towels, toilet paper, etc.
tube	toothpaste, hand cream, etc.

exercise 1 Write the correct counting unit under the picture of each type of food below. Some foods can have more than one counting unit.

a bag of sugar

__ ________ of soda

__ ________ of soup

__ ________ of milk

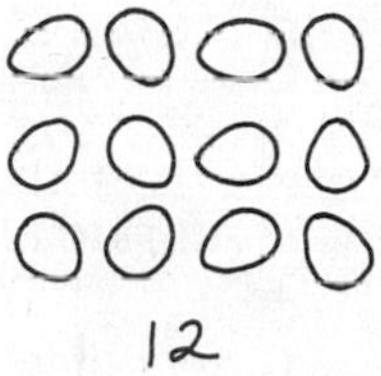

__ ________ eggs

__ ________ of lettuce

__ ________ of pickles

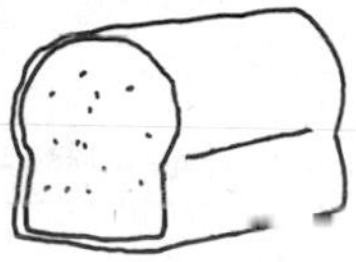

__ ________ of bread

cheese

__ ________ of cheese

cheese

__ ________ of cheese

exercise 2 Complete this grocery list.

Don't Forget

1. one gallon of milk	7. one ________ of lettuce
2. one ________ of potatoes	8. two ________ of toothpaste
3. two ________ of green onions	9. three ________ of hand soap
4. one ________ of mayonnaise	10. two ________ of bananas
5. three ________ of butter	11. one ________ of laundry detergent
6. one ________ eggs	12. one ________ of oil

activity 3 Change the eight items below on the left from metric units of measurement to basic units of measurement. Use the chart on the right to help you.

example: four liters of gas
Four liters of gas is about one gallon of gas.

METRIC UNITS

1. four liters of milk
2. ten centimeters of tape
3. one liter of juice
4. two meters of string
5. one kilo of chicken
6. 500 grams of coffee
7. five kilometers
8. 18 degrees Celsius

Basic Units

Length	meter = about 1.1 yards centimeter = .01 meter = about .4 inch kilometer = 1,000 meters = about .6 mile
Volume	liter = about 1.06 quarts (4 quarts = 1 gallon) milliliter = 0.001 liter 5 milliliters = 1 teaspoon
Weight	30 grams = 1.1 ounces kilogram = 1,000 grams = 2.2 pounds
Temperature	Celsius: 0°C = 32°F 37°F = 98.6°F

B. Questions with *how much*

How much + noncount noun + auxiliary verb + subject + verb

questions and possible answers	notes
How much bread should I buy? Buy two loaves of bread, please. **How much sugar** do we need? We need at least two bags.	Use *how much* in questions with noncount nouns.

exercise 4 Look at the pictures on page 233. How much of each ingredient do you need? Work with a partner. Take turns asking and answering questions with *how much.*

example: ice cream

A: **How much ice cream do I need?**

B: **You need two scoops of ice cream.**

1.

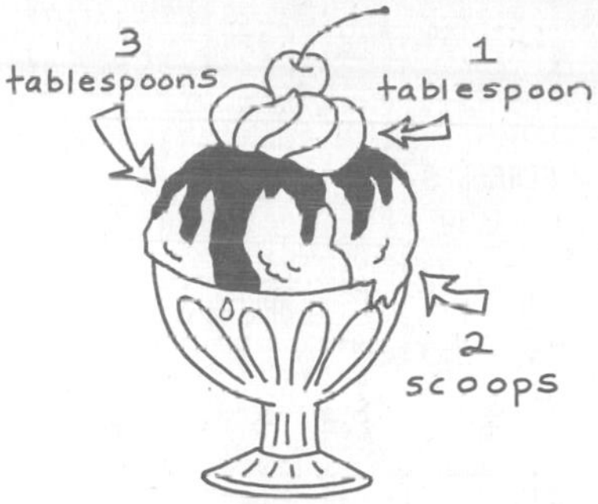

Ice-cream sundae
- ice cream
- chocolate sauce
- whipped cream

2.

Spaghetti for one
- cooked spaghetti
- spaghetti sauce
- grated cheese

3.

Grilled cheese sandwich
- bread
- cheese
- butter or margarine

4.

Tuna sandwich
- bread
- tuna
- chopped onion
- mayonnaise
- lettuce

exercise 5 Make fried rice for dinner. Work with a partner. Look at page 234. Student A looks at the list of ingredients. Ask Student B questions about the ingredients. Then Student B looks at the recipe card and answers Student A's questions.

example: oil

A: **How much oil do we need?**

B: **We need four tablespoons.**

STUDENT A

INGREDIENTS	
1. rice	5. celery
2. soy sauce	6. carrots
3. garlic	7. eggs
4. onions	8. chicken

STUDENT B

Chinese-American Fried Rice
(4 People)

4 tablespoons of soy sauce
2 teaspoons of mashed garlic
4 tablespoons of oil
1 small onion, chopped
2 stalks of celery, chopped
2 carrots, chopped
2 eggs, beaten
4 cups of cooked rice

Optional Ingredients

1 cup of beef, chicken, pork, or seafood, cut in strips

Mix soy sauce and garlic; set aside. Heat a frying pan and add oil. Fry any optional ingredients. Fry the rest of the ingredients in the order listed. Add rice and fry for two minutes. Add soy sauce and garlic. Fry for two more minutes. Serve hot.

Using What You've Learned

activity 1

Playing a Memory Game. Work in a chain. One student begins by saying, "We need *a bottle of ketchup*." The next student repeats the first item and adds one. Every student must repeat the list and add one item.

example: A: **We need a bottle of ketchup.**
B: **We need a bottle of ketchup and a dozen eggs.**
C: **We need a bottle of ketchup, a dozen eggs, and . . .**

activity 2

Explaining Recipes. Choose a favorite but simple recipe. Write a list of ingredients and directions for making it. Then work with a partner. Explain your recipe and read a list of ingredients to your partner. In a small group or as a class, share your recipes. Plan an international dinner if you wish!

TOPIC four

Common Noncount Nouns; a lot (of); a little Versus a few; not much Versus not many

Setting the Context

prereading questions

Look at the different types of food in the picture. Do you have these foods in your native country?

I'll Have a "Lite," Please

A Nowadays many North Americans are eating "lite" food. "Lite" food has less fat. People are changing their eating habits and choosing "lite" food, because it is not healthy to eat a lot of fat. As a result, supermarkets are carrying many kinds of low-fat products.

B A good example of these changes is milk. In the past, everyone drank "whole" milk. Nowadays, except for small children, not many people drink whole milk. Most adults drink 2 percent, 1 percent, or skim milk. There is a little fat in 2 percent and 1 percent milk, but skim milk has no fat.

C Milk is only one example. Just take a look in a few supermarkets. You will see "lite" food on every shelf. Throughout the country, supermarkets are selling—and shoppers are buying—low-fat, nonfat, lean, diet, or "lite" food.

discussion questions

1. What is "lite" food?
2. Why are Americans choosing "lite" food these days?
3. What kinds of milk can you find in supermarkets in the North America?

CULTURE NOTE

Many North Americans are very careful about fat in their diets. Do people in your country worry about fat? What do they worry about that might be in their food?

A. More Noncount Nouns

advice	**jewelry**	**pollution**	**bowling**
clothing	**laundry**	**time**	**cleaning**
crime	**mail**	**traffic**	**cooking**
furniture	**money**	**transportation**	**sewing**
help	**music**	**weather**	**swimming**
homework	**paper**	**work**	**tennis**
information			

Note: Some nouns such as *time* can be count or noncount nouns.

COUNT	I went there **many times.**
NONCOUNT	I have **some free time** this afternoon

B. *A lot (of)*

examples		notes
Count Nouns	***Noncount Nouns***	
I have **a lot of quarters** with me.	I have **a lot of change** with me.	Use *a lot of* with both count and noncount nouns.
Does he have **a lot?** He doesn't have **a lot.**	Does he have **a lot?** He doesn't have **a lot.**	Use *a lot* without a noun.

exercise 1 Work with a partner. Ask and answer questions with these cues. Give true answers.

example: eat / junk food

A: **Do you eat a lot of junk food?**
B: **Yes, I do.**
or **No, I don't eat a lot.**

1. eat / fruit
2. eat / vegetables
3. drink / coffee
4. spend / money last week
5. get / mail last week
6. have / American friends
7. have / problems when you came here
8. have / furniture in your home

C. A *little* Versus a *few*; *not much* versus *not many*

examples		notes
With Count Nouns		
Do you have **many quarters** with you?		Use *many* in questions with plural count nouns.
I have **a few quarters.** I do**n't** have **many quarters** with me.	(I have a small number, perhaps enough.) (I have a small number, probably not enough.)	Use *a few* and *not many* in statements with plural count nouns.
With Noncount Nouns		
Do you have **much change** with you?		Use *much* in questions with noncount nouns.
I have **a little change.** I do**n't** have **much change.**	(I have a small amount, perhaps enough.) (I have a small amount, probably not enough.)	Use *a little* and *not much* in statements with noncount nouns.

exercise 2 Use + *(some)* or – *(not enough)* to show the difference in meaning in these sentences.

examples: __+__ **She has a little money.**

__–__ **She doesn't have much money.**

1. _____ We have a little food at home.

_____ We don't have much juice.

2. _____ There are a few apples.

_____ We don't have many oranges.

3. _____ She has a few friends.

_____ He doesn't have many friends.

4. _____ We don't have much furniture in our apartment.

_____ They have a few chairs.

5. _____ He doesn't have much homework tonight.

_____ She has a few homework assignments tonight.

exercise 3 Complete this reading. Circle the correct words in parentheses. Circle *X* if no word is needed.

Diet and Eating Habits

A Around the world, people's eating habits are changing. In many ways, this is unfortunate. Traditional diets are often more healthy. For example, a traditional Japanese meal includes (a lot of / a lot) rice and vegetables and (a / a little)[1] fish. A traditional Mexican meal includes (some / a little)[2] beans and rice and (a few / a little)[3] tortillas. (A / X)[3] traditional Italian meal includes (some / a few)[4] fruit, (some / a little)[5] vegetables, and (a lot of / many)[6] pasta. All of these diets include (a / X)[7] healthy food.

B But traditional diets are changing. People in Tokyo, Mexico City, Rome, and (many / much)[8] other parts of the world are changing their eating habits. Today, (a / X)[9] hamburgers, hot dogs, and french fries are common around the world. People are eating (a lot of / a)[10] white bread instead of traditional food such as Colombian *arepas* or Mexican *tortillas*.

C In the United States, diets are changing too. Hopefully, the American diet will be better. In the past, (a / X)[11] traditional American dinner included (a lot of / a few)[12] meat, (much / some)[13] potatoes, and (a few / a little)[14] vegetables. Today Americans aren't eating as (many / much)[15] meat as in the past. They are also trying to eat (a few / a little)[16] fruit or (a few / a little)[17] vegetables at every meal. But Americans still eat (a lot of / many)[18] junk food too.

Today's Recommended Diet

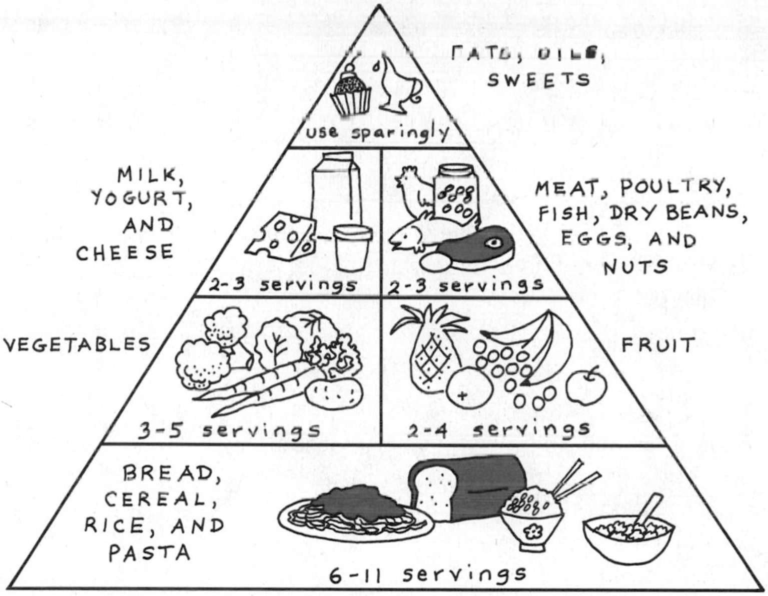

Using What You've Learned

activity

GROUP ACTIVITY

Discussing Diets. In a small group discuss these questions. Then choose one student to tell the class about the discussion.

1. What is the traditional diet in your country or culture?
2. Are diets changing? What are people in your country or culture eating nowadays?
3. What is your opinion about these changes?

checking your progress

Check your progress with structures from Chapters Seven and Eight. Be sure to review any problem areas.

Part 1. Choose the correct word(s) to complete each sentence.

1. Antonietta _____ a wonderful idea while she was riding the bus.
   a. has
   b. had
   c. having
   d. is having

2. When the doorbell rang, I _____ out of my seat.
   a. was jumping
   b. jump
   c. jumped
   d. jumping

3. Students in a new school often need _____ advice.
   a. a lot of
   b. many
   c. a lot
   d. a few

4. There weren't _____ people in the classroom, so it was easy to find a good seat.
   a. much
   b. some
   c. a lot
   d. many

5. While Juan and Silvia _____ to class last night, they saw an accident.
   a. are walking
   b. walked
   c. were walking
   d. walk

6. Pablo didn't have _____ eggs, so he couldn't bake a cake.
   a. any
   b. some
   c. much
   d. a lot

7. While Duc was studying, the telephone _____.
   a. rings
   b. is ringing
   c. was ringing
   d. rang

8. I don't have any money, but Jean has _____.
   a. much
   b. a lot of
   c. many
   d. a lot

9. When I turned on the computer, the electricity _____out.
   a. go
   b. went
   c. is going
   d. was going

10. Mari's class has many international students, but my class has only _____.
   a. a lot
   b. a lot of
   c. a little
   d. a few

Part 2. Circle the correct words to complete this story.

When I was a child, my parents (wanted / were wanting)[1] me to be healthy. They always gave me (much / a lot of)[2] milk, and they thought it was important to play in the sun. Today, doctors have very different ideas about good health, (do / don't)[3] they?

Mother's (use / used)[4] to give their babies "formula" and cow's milk. Now we know that mother's milk is better. In the past, parents also thought that children (have / had)[5] to eat meat every day. But many people do not eat (some / any)[6] meat, and they are very healthy.

Thirty years ago, (many / much)[7] people would sit in the sun for good health. Today, (a lot / a lot of)[8] people stay away from the sun because of the danger of skin cancer.

In the past, many older people (do / did)[9] not do (much / many)[10] exercise, but today there are exercise programs for everyone. Because of these new ideas, people now live longer and healthier lives.

CHAPTER nine

Travel and Leisure

in this chapter

Comparisons

Topic One:	Adjectives with *-ed* and *-ing*; *go* Versus *play; it's* + Adjective + Infinitive
Topic Two:	*Would rather;* Comparative Adjectives
Topic Three:	Adjectives Versus Adverbs; Comparative Adverbs; *as . . . as* with Adjectives and Adverbs
Topic Four:	Superlatives with Adjectives and Adverbs

TOPIC **one**

Adjectives with -ed and -ing; go Versus play; it's + Adjective + Infinitive

Setting the Context

prereading questions

Where is the young couple in this picture? How old do you think they are?

Josh

A Hi. My name is Josh. I'm a student. I grew up in Naples, Florida. I studied biology at the community college there for two years. I still study biology, but I'm not in Florida anymore. I'm at the University of Texas at Austin. We call it UT.

B My life is different here—very different. For one thing, UT is much bigger than my old community college. And Austin is a lot more exciting than Naples. It's great to go out at night here. I mean there are just more things to do—more movies, more music, more parties.

C Yeah, this is an interesting place, and I am never bored, but I still miss home.

discussion questions

Circle T (True) or F (False). Correct the false sentences.

1. T F Josh used to live in Naples, Florida.

2. T F UT is smaller than his old community college.

3. T F Austin is more exciting than Naples.

4. T F It's great to stay home at night.

5. T F Josh is never bored.

CULTURE NOTE

Josh comes from Florida but is now studying in Texas. It is common for college students in the U.S. to study far from their homes. It is also common to start at one college and then transfer to another. Some students will study at four or more colleges before graduating!

exercise 1

Complete this reading with the present, past, and past continuous tenses of the verbs in parentheses.

Hi! This __is__ (be) Josh again. I ___1___ (want to) tell you about my girlfriend. Her name ___2___ (be) Michelle.

Michelle and I ___3___ (be) really happy together. We ___4___ (have) the same major, so we ___5___ (study) together. That really ___6___ (help) me because she ___7___ (be) very intelligent. But it ___8___ (be) funny. We ___9___ (have) different opinions about what to do for fun. She ___10___ (like) to do one thing. I ___11___ (like) to do another.

For example, last night I ___12___ (ask) Michelle to go to a movie with me. She ___13___ (say) OK. Then while we ___14___ (walk) to the movie, she ___15___

(change) her mind. She _____ (say) that she _____ (want) to go to a concert. Of
16 17

course, I _____ (agree) to go to the concert. Well, it _____ (be) really boring. I
18 19

_____ (be) bored after five minutes. But Michelle _____ (love) it. She _____
20 21 22

(say) that it _____ (be) the best concert this year!
23

We just _____ (have) very different opinions.
24

A. Adjectives with *-ing* and *-ed*

Adjectives with *-ing* and *-ed* often follow *to be.*

examples		notes
Giver Receiver The movie **excited** Josh.	The movie was **excit*ing*.** Josh was **excit*ed*.**	Use *-ing* with the *giver* of a feeling.
Giver Receiver Dave **bores** Michelle.	Dave is **bor*ing*.** Michelle is **bor*ed*.**	Use *-ed* with the *receiver* of a feeling.

exercise 2 Change each underlined verb to an adjective. Use the *-ed* or *-ing* form of the adjective to complete the sentences.

I'm Michelle. Josh told you we often have different opinions of things. Well, it's true. For example:

1. We watched a TV show last night.

It excited me. For me, the show was ______exciting______. I was ______excited______.

It bored Josh. For Josh, the show was ____________________. He was ____________________.

2. We both read the same book.

The book fascinated me. I was ____________________. The book was ____________________.

The book shocked Josh. He was ____________________. The book was ____________________.

3. We went to eat at a restaurant.

The food disappointed me. The food was ______________________. I was ______________________.

The food satisfied Josh. The food was ______________________. He was ______________________.

4. We went to a football game.

The game confused me. I was ______________________. The game was ______________________.

The game excited Josh. He was ______________________. The game was ______________________.

5. We went to hear a politician speak.

The politician surprised me. The politician was ______________________. I was ______________________.

The politician didn't interest Josh. The politician was not ______________. Josh was not ______________________.

exercise 3 Here's one thing Josh and I agree on. It's fun to watch people, especially in our classes. It's entertaining, and it doesn't cost anything!

Look at the pictures below and on page 246. Then answer the questions using the *-ing* or *-ed* forms of the adjectives.

example: Who is bored?

The students are bored.

1. Who is bored? Who is boring?

2. Who is interesting? Who is interested?

3. Who was fascinated?
Who was fascinating?

4. Who was disappointed?
What was disappointing?

5. Who is surprised?
What is surprising?

6. Is the food disappointing or disappointed? Is Josh disappointing or disappointed?

7. Is the book confused or confusing? How about Harry?

B. Using *go* with an Activity

Go* + verb + *-ing

examples	notes
I **went shopping** yesterday. I'm going to **go jogging** tomorrow.	The verb *go* is followed by the activity. The activity ends in *-ing.*

Using *play* with Games and Sports

examples	notes
Let's **play** tennis. I **play** cards almost every night.	The verb *play* is followed by the name of the game or sport. The *-ing* ending is *not* used.

exercise 4 Follow the pattern below with a partner. Use *go* or *play* in your answers. Change roles.

example: football / bowl

A: **What do you want to do this afternoon?**
B: **Let's play football.**
A: **No, let's go bowling.**

1. shop / tennis
2. roller-skate / chess
3. Ping-Pong / ski
4. jog / checkers
5. surf / baseball
6. soccer / sightsee
7. dance / basketball
8. soccer / walk

C. It's + Adjective + Infinitive

People often use this pattern to give an opinion about an activity or game.

examples	notes
It's great to play cards. **It's boring to go** jogging. **It's terrible to be** sick.	Adjectives such as *fascinating, exciting, interesting,* and *tiring* are commonly used in this pattern.

exercise 5 Look at the list of ten activities on page 248. Give your opinion of these activities by checking the appropriate boxes. Then work with a partner. Take turns making sentences. In your sentences, you can also use words like *sometimes, usually, always,* and *never.*

example: to stay home

It's sometimes boring to stay home because there's nobody to talk with.

	Great	Fantastic	Fun	Boring	Tiring	Terrible
1. to stay home				√		
2. to watch TV						
3. to go shopping						
4. to read a book						
5. to go to a museum						
6. to visit the library						
7. to go to the movies						
8. to go swimming						
9. to play tennis						
10. to go to a party						

Using What You've Learned

activity

GROUP ACTIVITY

Giving Opinions. Write six things that you often do. Then, in a small group, share your opinions of each other's activities. Use *it's interesting / boring / fascinating,* and so on. Give the reason for your opinion.

example: hiking*

In my opinion, it's fascinating to go hiking because I love nature.

1. ______________________________

2. ______________________________

3. ______________________________

4. ______________________________

5. ______________________________

6. ______________________________

**hiking* walking in the mountains or woods for fun

TOPIC two
Would rather; Comparative Adjectives

Setting the Context

prereading questions

Look at the picture. What is the man thinking about?

Decisions, Decisions

DALE: Hey, Jack. I heard you and Julie sold your business.
JACK: Yeah, we want to take some time off. There are more interesting things to do than just work.
DALE: What are you going to do?
JACK: Travel, but we can't decide between Italy and France. I'd rather go to France than Italy. Julie would rather visit Italy. Hey, you know Europe well. What do you think?
DALE: Well, I love both countries. But in my opinion, Italy has better museums than France, and it's usually cheaper. Also, Italian is easier to speak than French. On the other hand, France has more beautiful churches than Italy. And I think French food is a little better than Italian.
JACK: So which country should we visit?
DALE: Both!

discussion questions

Circle T (True) or F (False). Correct the false sentences.

1. T F Jack just bought a new business.
2. T F Jack wants to go to Italy, not France.
3. T F Julie doesn't agree with Jack.
4. T F Dale thinks Italy has more museums than France.
5. T F Dale thinks France has more churches than Italy.

A. *Would rather*

Use *would rather* if there is a choice. *Would rather* shows preference.

examples	notes
Would you **rather** visit China or Japan? I **'d** (I **would**) **rather** visit Japan. **Would** they **rather** come tonight or tomorrow? They **'d** (They **would**) **rather** come tonight (than tomorrow).	In statements, *would* is usually shortened (*I'd, He'd, They'd,* etc.). *Than* may be used to show the choice you do not prefer.

exercise 1

Imagine you are like Jack. You have free time and a lot of money. Use *would rather* to answer these questions.

example: Would you rather go to France or Italy?
I'd rather go to France (than Italy).

1. Would you rather speak French or Italian?
2. Would you rather visit Thailand or Singapore?
3. Would you rather see Brazil or Peru?
4. Would you rather eat Mexican food or American food?
5. Would you rather go to Spain or Morocco?
6. Would you rather read a book or watch a movie?
7. Would you rather study more or take a break?
8. Would you rather listen to jazz or rock and roll?

exercise 2 With a partner, take turns asking and answering these questions with *would rather.* Use the cues to form the questions. Then add questions of your own.

example: learn Arabic or English

Would you rather learn Arabic or English?
I'd rather learn Arabic.

1. see a rock concert or an opera
2. live in Spain or Portugal
3. play soccer or ____________
4. visit Egypt or ____________
5. eat ____________ or ____________
6. watch ____________ or ____________
7. ____________ ____________ or ____________
8. ____________ ____________ or ____________
9. ____________ ____________ or ____________
10. ____________ ____________ or ____________

B. Comparative Adjectives (1)

Comparatives show how two things are different. The form of the comparative depends on how many syllables the adjective has.

	examples	notes
One-Syllable Adjectives	France isn't **cheap.** Italy is **cheaper than** France.	Add *-er* to one-syllable adjectives. Use *than* to show the other choice.
Adjectives That End in y	French isn't **easy.** Italian is **easier** to learn **than** French.	When adjectives end in *y,* change the *y* to *i* and add *-er.*

exercise 3 Jack and Julie are going to visit both France and Italy. Which cities should they visit? Study the map of France on page 252 and use your imagination. Then use the adjectives on page 252 to make sentences comparing the cities.

In France—Paris or Nice

example: cool

Paris is cooler than Nice.

1. warm	**6.** close (to the ocean)
2. noisy	**7.** sunny
3. green	**8.** cloudy
4. big	**9.** near (to England)
5. small	

C. Comparative Adjectives (2)

Longer adjectives use *more . . . than* to form the comparative.

	examples	notes
Two-Syllable Adjectives That Don't End in y	This map is **more helpful than** that one. She is **more tired than** Jack.	Use *more . . . than* with these adjectives. Don't add *-er.*
Adjectives with More Than Two Syllables	The mountains are **more beautiful than** the beach.	Use *more . . . than* with these adjectives. Don't add *-er.*

exercise 4 What about Italy? Which Italian cities should Jack and Julie visit? Read what the travel agent has to say. Then use the adjectives below to make sentences comparing Florence and Rome.

In Italy Florence or Rome

example: beautiful

Florence is more beautiful than Rome.

ROME
FLORENCE
Rome is important, exciting, and interesting, but it is also crowded.
Florence is beautiful, relaxing, peaceful, and safe, but it is also very expensive.

1. exciting
2. safe
3. expensive
4. important
5. relaxing
6. interesting
7. crowded
8. peaceful
9. enjoyable

exercise 5 With a partner, choose two cities that you both know well. Then use these adjectives to compare the two cities. Add two adjectives of your own.

1. beautiful
2. big
3. exciting
4. noisy
5. small
6. interesting
7. dangerous
8. smoggy
9. entertaining
10. wet
11. ___________
12. ___________

D. Irregular Comparative Adjectives

Some comparative adjectives do not follow the rules on pages 251 and 252. They are irregular. Here are three common examples.

adjective → comparative	examples
good → **better**	Mary is **better than** Dave in sports.
bad → **worse**	Dave is **worse than** Mary in sports.
far → **farther**	Mary can run **farther than** Dave.

exercise 6

Part 1: Jack and Julie finally decided to visit Paris and Florence, but how should they travel? Use the comparative forms of the verbs in parentheses to complete the conversation.

JACK: We know that we are going to Europe. But how should we get there? Is it ___better___ (good) to sail or to fly?

JULIE: For me, flying is ______________ (good) than sailing.
1

JACK: Why do you say that?

JULIE: Flying is ______________ (fast). It's also ______________
2 3
(cheap), and it's ______________ (safe) than sailing.
4

JACK: I disagree. For me, flying is ______________ (bad) than sailing. Sailing
5
may be ______________ (slow) and ______________ (expen-
6 7
sive) than flying. But sailing is also ______________ (interesting), and it's
8
______________ romantic.
9

Part 2: The conversation continues. Again fill in the correct comparative forms. But this time, finish the dialogue.

JACK: Should we travel by car or by train in Europe?

JULIE: For me, the train is ______________ (good) than the car.
1

JACK: Why do you say that?

JULIE: The train is ______________ (good) because ______________
2
____
3

JACK: I disagree. For me, the train is ______________ (bad) than the car.
4

JULIE: Why?

JACK: The train is ______________ (bad) because ______________
5
____
6

Using What You've Learned

activity 1

Talking About the U.S. and Canada. How well do you know the U.S. and Canada? With a partner, fill in as many cities on the map as you can. Then use *closer* and *farther* to ask and answer questions about these cities.

example: Which is farther from here, San Francisco or Reno?
San Francisco is farther.

activity 2

Planning a Trip. You and a friend are planning a trip. However, you cannot agree on a place. You visit your travel agent and ask for help. Your travel agent can tell you the good points and bad points of each place. In groups of three—you, your friend, and the travel agent—role-play this situation. Use one of the pairs of vacations below or choose your own.

1. a ski trip to Colorado versus a sightseeing trip to New York City
2. an African safari versus a mountain-climbing expedition to Mount Everest
3. a backpacking trip in Nepal versus a luxury cruise on the Mediterranean

TOPIC three
Adjectives Versus Adverbs; Comparative Adverbs; as . . . as with Adjectives and Adverbs

Setting the Context

prereading questions

What did the man in the picture just do? How old do you think he is?

The Prime of Life

A My name is John Wilson. I'm a professor at a small university in Vermont. My teaching schedule keeps me pretty busy, so I really enjoy my time away from work. What do I do for fun? Lots of things! I go to movies, plays, and concerts. I sing in a choir and play the piano. But more than anything, I love to exercise. That's my idea of entertainment!

B I love any kind of sport. I run, bicycle, ski, and play tennis, but basketball is my favorite. There is just one problem. I'm not as young as I used to be. I run more slowly than I used to. I can't jump as high. And I get hurt more easily. For all these reasons, I don't play as well as I did a few years ago. Oh well, I guess that's just part of getting older.

discussion questions Circle T (True) or F (False). Correct the false sentences.

1. T F John Wilson is musical.
2. T F He enjoys exercise.
3. T F He runs faster than he used to.
4. T F He can't jump as high as he used to.
5. T F He plays better than he used to.

A. Adjectives and Adverbs

	examples	notes
Adjectives	John is a **slow** runner. John is **slow.** Dave is a **fast** runner. Dave is **fast.**	Adjectives describe nouns.
Adverbs	John runs **slowly**. Dave runs **quickly**.	Adverbs describe actions. Most adverbs end in *-ly.*
One-Syllable Adverb	Dave runs **fast.** He works **hard.** He worked **late** last night.	The words *fast, hard,* and *late* have the same form for adjective and adverb. Do *not* add *-ly.*
Irregular Adverbs	Susan is a **good** soccer player. Susan plays soccer **well.**	The correct adverb form of *good* is *well.*

exercise 1 Circle the correct forms, adjective or adverb, in the pairs of sentences.

1. John is a (good / well) player. John plays basketball (good / well)
2. He is a (slow / slowly) runner. He runs (slow / slowly).
3. John jumps (good / well). He is a (good / well) jumper.
4. His voice is (soft / softly). He speaks (soft / softly).
5. John plays (careful / carefully). He is a (careful / carefully) player.
6. He doesn't play (dangerous / dangerously). He isn't a (dangerous / dangerously) player.
7. He is a (beautiful / beautifully) singer. He sings (beautiful / beautifully).

8. John walks (quiet / quietly). He is a (quiet / quietly) walker.

9. John gets hurt (easy / easily). It's (easy / easily) to hurt him.

10. John thinks (fast / fast). He is a (fast / fast) thinker.

11. John plays the piano (good / well). He is a (good / well) pianist.

B. Comparative Adverbs

Comparative adverbs show the difference between two actions. The form of the comparative depends on how many syllables the adverb has.

	examples	notes
One-Syllable Adverbs	John's son runs **faster than** John.	Use *-er . . . than* with these adverbs.
Adverbs with Two or More Syllables	John finished his work **more quickly than** Ben.	Use *more* (not *-er*) with these adverbs.
Irregular Adverbs	Susan plays tennis **better than** John. She can also run **farther than** John.	Irregular adverbs have the same form as irregular adjectives.

exercise 2

Ben and John are friends. They do a lot of things together. Ben is better than John in many things. Write sentences using the cues and the pictures.

examples: (early) *Ben finishes earlier than John (does).*
(late) *John finishes later than Ben (does).*

1.

a. (hard) ____________________

b. (good) ____________________

c. (bad) ____________________

2.

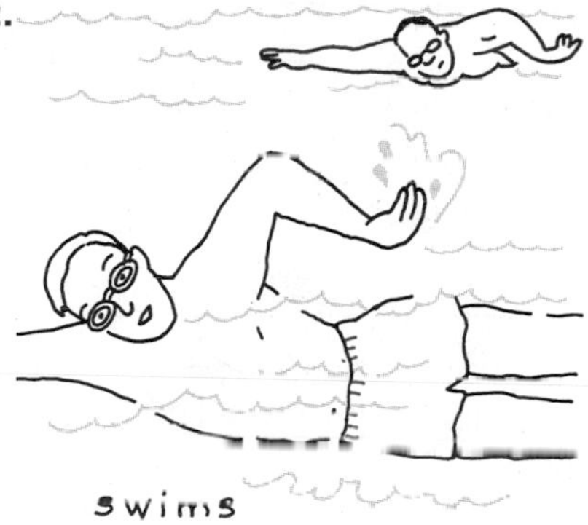

a. (fast) ____________________

b. (slow) ____________________

c. (quick) ____________________

3.

a. (dangerous) ____________________

b. (safe) ____________________

c. (careful) ____________________

4.

a. (far) ____________________

b. (hard) ____________________

c. (serious) ____________________

C. Comparisons with (*not*) *as . . . as*

As . . . as shows that two people, situations, or things are the same in some way. *Not as . . . as* shows that the first person situation, or thing is less or smaller in some way than the second.

examples

As + adjective + as	John is **as intelligent as** Patty. (They are equal.) He is**n't as intelligent as** Albert. (Albert is more intelligent.)
As + Adverb + as	John plays chess **as slowly as** Dave. (They are equal.) John does**n't** sing **as well as** he used to. (He used to sing better.)

exercise 3 Dave is another one of John's friends. Dave does everything about as well as John. With a partner, fill in the correct forms of the words in parentheses. Then take turns asking and answering the questions. Use *as . . . as* in your answers.

example: How ___far___ (far) can Dave run?

Dave can run _as far as John_.

1. How __________ (fast) can Dave run? Dave can run ______________.
2. How __________ (good) can Dave run? Dave can run ______________.
3. How __________ (careful) does Dave ski? Dave skis ______________.
4. How __________ (good) does Dave ski? Dave skis ______________.
5. How __________ (dangerous) does Dave ski? Dave skis ______________ ______________________________________.
6. How __________ (quick) does Dave learn? Dave learns ______________.
7. How __________ (clear) does he write? Dave writes ______________.
8. How __________ (good) does he speak? Dave speaks ______________.

exercise 4

Similes are sayings that compare two things. Similies often use *as* + adjective + *as*. Match the words on the left with the expressions on the right. Then make sentences with *as* . . . *as*. Use members of your class for the subjects.

example: **Fabio is as stubborn as a mule.**

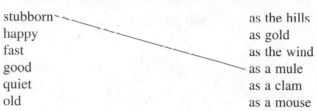

stubborn	as the hills
happy	as gold
fast	as the wind
good	as a mule
quiet	as a clam
old	as a mouse

exercise 5

I'm Susan. I'm married to John Wilson. We got married twenty years ago. He has changed in some ways in twenty years, and I have too. Fill in the correct forms of the words on the left.

1. (handsome) John isn't as ___handsome___ as he used to be. In other words, he used to be ___more handsome___.
2. (lazy) I am not as ________________ as I used to be. In other words, I used to be ________________.
3. (good) John doesn't play basketball as ________________ as he used to. In other words, he used to play ________________.
4. (bad) He isn't as ________________ at cards as he used to be. In other words, he used to be ________________.
5. (slow) I don't swim as ________________ as I used to. In other words, I used to swim ________________.
6. (good) I am not as ________________ at other sports as I used to be. In other words, I used to be ________________ at sports.
7. (quick) John doesn't run as ________________ as he used to. In other words, he used to run ________________.
8. (careless) He isn't as ________________ as he used to be. In other words, he used to be ________________.

exercise 6 Complete this reading. Circle the correct forms of the words in parentheses.

You're As (Young / Younger) As You Feel

Hi! I'm Mel. I'm John's father. I used to work in a factory. I was a welder. My job was (more hard / hardly / harder)[1] than most other jobs, but it was (more interesting / more interested)[2] too. I worked (quickly / quicker / more quickly)[3] and also (careful / carefully / more carefully)[4] than other workers. My work was (good / more good / better)[5] than most of the other welders. Anyway, that doesn't matter now. I am retired.

What do I do with my free time? A lot! Some retired people are (bored / boring)[6]. That's because they have (bored / boring)[7] lives. They sit around the house and don't do anything. It's their own fault, if you ask me.

It's true. I am not as (young / younger / more young)[8] as I used to be. So what? My life is never (bored / boring)[9]. It's easy (find / to find)[10] things to do. I (go / play)[11] cards, I (watch / see)[12] TV, and I (go / play)[13] bowling. It's always fun (read / to read)[14], (work / to work)[15] in my garden, and (to go / to play)[16] tennis. Oh, yeah. Another thing, I love to travel. How could I possibly be (bored / boring)[17]? Your life is as (good / well)[18] as you make it.

CULTURE NOTE

Mel likes to be independent. Older people in the United States usually like to be independent. Some older people live with their sons and daughters, but most like to live on their own. There are also special retirement communities—groups of houses or apartments for older people—in the United States. You have to be more than sixty years old to live in one of these communities.

Using What You've Learned

activity 1

Writing About Changes. How many changes will you feel when you are old? Imagine you are seventy years old. Work with a partner. Make at least ten groups of sentences like those in exercise 5. You may use the list of words in exercise 5, but be sure to add some of your own.

activity 2

GROUP ACTIVITY

Talking About Retirement. Discuss these questions with a partner or in small groups.

1. Do you know any people who are retired?
2. Are their lives exciting or boring?
3. Do they enjoy life more now than when they were working?
4. What do they do with their free time?
5. When you retire, what will your life be like?
6. Are you worried about getting old?

activity 3

GROUP ACTIVITY

Similies. Do you have similies in your native language? Work in small groups. Try to work in a group with people from your country. Translate similies from your language into English. Then, share your similies with the class. Are your similies similar? Are they different?

TOPIC four

Superlatives with Adjectives and Adverbs

Setting the Context

prereading questions

How old is the woman in the picture? Where is she? What do you think happened to her?

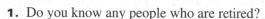

Laid Up

A My name is Esther. I am usually very active, but I had a car accident three weeks ago. I broke my leg. Now I'm going to be in this cast for at least two more months.

B How do I entertain myself? I read. I listen to the radio. But for me, the most interesting thing is TV. In fact, TV is so interesting that I often watch it more than five hours a day.

C I watch everything—news, game shows, movies, musical performances, MTV, and sports. Then I compare many of the actors, musicians, dancers, and athletes that I see.

discussion questions

Circle T (True) or F (False). Correct the false sentences.

1. T F Esther had a skiing accident.
2. T F She reads five hours a day.
3. T F The most interesting thing for Esther is radio.
4. T F TV is so boring she never watches it.
5. T F She watches many types of shows.

A. Superlatives with Adjectives and Adverbs

Use superlatives to compare three or more people or things. Use *the* with superlatives.

	examples	notes
One-Syllable Adjectives and Adverbs	I am **the fastest** runner on our team. Joe runs **the slowest** of anyone.	Add *-est* to one-syllable adjectives and adverbs. Use *the* before the superlative.
Two-Syllable Adjectives Ending in y	Jack is **the laziest** person on the team.	Add *-est* to two-syllable adjectives ending in *y*.

Longer Adjectives and Adverbs	Watching TV is **the most interesting** thing to do. Esther is **the most dangerous** skier I know. She skis **the most dangerously** of anyone.	Use *the most* with multisyllable adjectives (not ending in *y*). Use *the most* with all multisyllable adverbs.
Irregulars	Janis skis **the best** of anyone I know. She is **the worst** student in our school.	The superlative form of *good* is *best* . The superlative form of *bad* is *worst.*

exercise 1 Hi, I'm Esther. Last week I saw these three actors on late-night movies. Use the pictures and your imagination to answer the questions on the next page. Use the superlative in your answers.

Vern

Gary

George

example: Who is the most handsome of the three?
(I think that) Gary is the most handsome (of the three).

1. Who looks the strongest?
2. Who looks the most intelligent?
3. Who looks the dumbest?
4. Who is the most athletic?
5. Who is the youngest?
6. Who is the heaviest?
7. Who is the best actor?
8. Who is the worst actor?

exercise 2 I also saw these three actresses. Use your knowledge and your imagination to answer these questions.

example: Is Penny more famous than Eva?

No, Eva is more famous than Penny.

1. Who is the most famous?
2. Is Eva prettier than Penny?
3. Who is the prettiest?
4. Is Penny as old as Suzanne?
5. Who is the oldest?
6. Is Eva as thin as Suzanne?
7. Who is the thinnest?
8. Does Penny look as athletic as Eva?
9. Who looks the most athletic?
10. Who is the best actress?
11. Who is the worst actress?

B. Comparatives and Superlatives Used Together

The same sentence can have both the comparative and the superlative. This happens when more than two people or things are compared.

> Julie is **happier than** Joan, but Laura is **the happiest** of the three.
> Ahmad plays football **better than** Harry, but Tony plays **the best.**
> Dave is **more serious than** Kevin, but Bill is **the most serious** of the three.

exercise 3 On Sunday, there were three games on TV—a baseball game, a soccer game, and an American football game. Write your opinion of these sports.

example: (fast) *Football is faster than baseball, but soccer is the fastest of the three.*

1. (slow) ______________________________
2. (interesting) ______________________________
3. (exciting) ______________________________
4. (boring) ______________________________

5. (dangerous) ______________________________

6. (safe) ______________________________

7. (good) ______________________________

exercise 4 Last week there was a detective show on TV. It was called "Detective Maggot." The show began with the star (Detective Maggot) speaking. Circle the correct forms in parentheses.

My name is Maggot. I live (in / on) Kansas City. I'm a cop. Kansas City is like most cities. It has (good / well)[1] people, and it has (bad / badly)[2] people. My job is to catch the bad ones. It's a (dirty / dirtier)[3] job, but someone has to do it. Let me tell you about my last case.

It was Monday about noon. I got a call from a woman. Teresa was her name. . . . No, it was Amanda. That's right, Amanda. I can forget her name, but I (never could / could never)[4] forget her. Amanda was (frightened / frightening)[5]. She said her husband (is / was)[6] trying to kill her. I met her at 1:00 P.M. in her hotel lobby.

When I saw her, I was (shocking / shocked)[7]. She was (beautiful / more beautiful)[8]. She was (more / as)[9] beautiful as any movie star. She was (more beautiful / beautifuller)[10] than any model. She was (as beautiful / the most beautiful)[11] woman in the world. Hey, what can I say? She was beautiful!

She told me her story. She said her husband (is / was)[12] very powerful. She said he (doesn't / didn't)[13] love her anymore. She said he (is / was)[14] trying to poison her. Then she told me her (husband / husband's)[15] name. It was Ralph Smiley. I almost fell over. He was the mayor of our city!

Late that night, I went to the mayor's house. I entered through a window. I walked (quick / quickly)[16] toward the living room. When I got there, I couldn't

(believe / believed) [17] my eyes. The mayor was (in / on) [18] the floor. There was blood (in / on) [19] the rug. He was dead! Next to the body, there was a note.

Using What You've Learned

activity 1

Talking About Sports. With a partner, choose three different sports. Make a list of seven adjectives. Then make comparisons like those in exercise 3. Be sure to use both comparatives and superlatives in your sentences.

activity 2

Talking About Famous People. Work with a partner. Who are the most famous people you can think of? Choose two people, and write their names in the blanks 1 and 2 below. Write the name of a student in your class in the blank 3. Then use the adjectives on page 269 to write comparisons of the three people.

1. ______________________ **2.** ______________________ **3.** ______________________

famous people — other student

example: (athletic)

Michael Jordan is more athletic than Princess Diana, but Ana is the most athletic of the three.

ADJECTIVES

1. (good-looking) ______________________________

____

2. (rich) ______________________________

____

3. (lazy) ______________________________

____

4. (intelligent) ______________________________

____

5. (famous) ______________________________

____

6. (exciting) ______________________________

____

activity 3

Writing and Telling Stories. From exercise 4, you know part of Maggot's story. But there is much more. What did the note say? Who killed Mayor Smiley? Why? Can Detective Maggot find the murderer? With a partner, finish this story with at least seven sentences. Then retell your story to the class. Use both adjectives and adverbs as you retell the story. Also, try to use the following structures at least once: *as . . . as, -er* or *more . . . than, -est* or *the most.*

____

____

____

____

____

____

____

____

____

____

____

____

____

CHAPTER ten

Our Planet

in this chapter

Common Uses of the Past Participle

TOPIC one
Overview of Past Participles

Setting the Context

prereading questions Look at the pictures and describe them. What do they have in common?

Life on Our Planet

A Life on our planet is incredibly varied. When you think about the varieties of life here, you will be amazed. Almost 6 billion people live on earth. More than fifteen hundred languages and thousands of cultures exist around the world. But we humans are only a part of life on earth. Millions of plants, animals, insects, and birds also populate our planet.

B Unfortunately, humans are often destructive to other living things. Consider the following:

- At least 36 species of mammals* are now extinct.
- At least 120 species of mammals are in danger of extinction.
- At least 350 species of birds are endangered.
- Estimates are that 20,000 plant species are endangered.

C Statistics like these frighten us because when a species dies, it will never return. Many people are concerned about protecting all life on earth, and they work hard to stop more damage from happening. However, other people are convinced that our planet is already damaged beyond repair. What do you think?

discussion questions

1. What does *extinction* mean?
2. Do you know of any endangered animals or plants? Share some examples.
3. What does *damaged beyond repair* mean?

A. Past Participles with Verbs of Emotion

For regular verbs, the past participle is the same as the simple past tense (verb + *-ed*). We use the past participle of many verbs to describe our emotions or feelings. A variety of prepositions can follow the past participle. See Chapter Nine for more information on other forms of these verbs.

Subject + verb	Subject + *be* + past participle
The test worries me.	I **am worried** about the test.
The instructions confuse me.	I **am confused** by the instructions.

verbs	past participles	verbs	past participles
amaze	**amazed (at)**	**frighten**	**frightened (by)**
bore	**bored (with)**	**frustrate**	**frustrated (with)**
concern	**concerned (about)**	**interest**	**interested (in)**
confuse	**confused (about)**	**please**	**pleased (with)**
convince	**convinced (about)**	**satisfy**	**satisfied (with)**
determine	**determined (to)**	**sadden**	**saddened (about)**
disappoint	**disappointed (about)**	**scare**	**scared (of)**
disgust	**disgusted (about)**	**shock**	**shocked (about)**
excite	**excited (about)**	**surprise**	**surprised (about)**
exhaust	**exhausted (from)**	**tire**	**tired (of)**
		worry	**worried (about)**

**mammals* warm-blooded animals that produce milk for their babies

exercise 1 Complete the reading by circling the correct words in parentheses.

WORKING TO PROTECT THE ENVIRONMENT

My name is Stella, and I am (concern / concerned)[1] about environmental issues. I am (convince / convinced)[2] that our planet is in trouble.

Many things (worry / worried)[3] me. Air and water pollution in our major cities (scare / scared)[4] me. I am (frighten / frightened)[5] about changes in our weather. And I am (sadden / saddened)[6] about the animals and plants around the world that are (endanger / endangered)[7].

Do environmental issues (worry / worried)[8] you? If you are (worry / worried)[9], do something about it. Don't just be (concerned / concerning)[10]. Try to help! Our planet is home to all life here, not just humans. If you are (interest / interested)[11], join us today!

exercise 2 Rewrite these sentences to use past participles.

example: Environmental issues worry many people.
Many people are worried about environmental issues.

1. The large animals in Africa worry many people.

____

2. Learning about African wildlife interests Lou.

____

3. Protecting wildlife concerns many zoos and nature preserves.

____

4. At the zoo, the lion frightened the little boy.

____

5. Seeing a tiger excited the little girl.

____

6. Spending the whole day at the zoo exhausted the mother.

____

B. *Be* and *get* + Past Participle

We often use past participles in expressions with *be* and *get*. *Get* has the meaning of *become*. Topic Three of this chapter gives more information on the verb *be* with past participles (passive voice forms of verbs).

Subject + *be* + past participle	**Subject + *get* + past participle**
I'**m bored**. Let's go to a movie.	Children often **get bored** on rainy days.
Jack **was confused** about the assignment.	I **get confused** when people speak fast.
She **is tired** because she stayed up late.	Because of her illness, she **gets tired** easily.

exercise 3 Complete these sentences in your own words.

1. Sometimes I get concerned about . . .
2. My family often gets worried about . . .
3. I often get confused about . . .
4. Sometimes I get disappointed about . . .
5. I really get tired of . . .
6. I am (not) satisfied with . . .
7. I am pleased with . . .
8. I am excited about . . .

C. Common Expressions with Past Participles

Here are common expressions that use past participles. Some of these verbs are regular, and the past participle has the *-ed* ending. Others are irregular and may change spelling and/or pronunciation. Topic Two gives more information on irregular forms, and Appendix Three (pages 308 and 309) gives a list of the most common irregular verbs in English.

verbs	past participles	examples
arrest	arrested	The criminal **was arrested** by the police.
break	broken	The front window is **broken.**
build	built	That house is very well **built.**
close	closed	The library is **closed** now.
damage	damaged	The table was **damaged,** but now it's fixed.
drink	drunk	The man got **drunk** at the party.
(re)elect	(re)elected	The mayor was **reelected** last month.
endanger	endangered	Many animals are **endangered.**
finish	finished	Is your homework **finished?**
go	gone	There's no more sugar. It's all **gone.**
hurt	hurt	Martin got **hurt** during the soccer game.
know	(well) known	That actor is very well **known.**
involve	involved	He's not **involved** in that project.
lose	lost	I got **lost** on the way to your house.
pollute	polluted	That river is very **polluted.**
shut	shut	Are all the doors **shut?**
upset	upset	She was **upset** about her bad grades.
vary	varied	Her problems are **varied.**
write	(well) written	That paper was very well **written.**

verbs	past participles	examples
divorce	divorced from	He got **divorced from** his wife in 1984.
engage	engaged to	When did Susan get **engaged to** her boyfriend?
marry	married to	Mary got **married to** Charles in Las Vegas.
separate	separated from	Diane **separated from** her husband last month.

exercise 4 This is the beginning of the story of Sam Sleeze. Write the past participles in the blanks in each section.

1.

married	invited	elected	engaged ✓	interested

In 1980, Sam Sleeze got engaged (1) to his girlfriend, and in 1981, the couple got ______ (2) in a large wedding in Corrupt Town. All of the important people in town were ______ (3) to the wedding because Sam was ______ (4) in politics. He was hoping to get ______ (5) mayor.

2.

broken	drunk	hurt	arrested

At the wedding, there was a lot of alcohol and many people got ______ (6). One man fell off a chair and got ______ (7). Another man's arm was ______ (8) because he fell off a table. Finally, the police came and several guests were ______ (9).

3.

interested	upset	disappointed

During the wedding day, Sam's new wife Sue was ______ (10) and ______ (11) because Sam did not stay with her and forgot about her. He was ______ (12) in getting money for his political campaign.

4.

reelected	separated	divorced	finished

Sam and Sue Sleeze did not have a happy life together, and after Sam's election as mayor, the couple got ______ (13). When Sam's first term as mayor was ______ (14), he decided to run for mayor again. When Sam got ______ (15), Sue filed for divorce. They got ______ (16) in 1990.

5. | built | polluted | determined | worried |

While he was mayor, Sam became very rich. At the same time, many new factories were ____________ (17) in Corrupt Town. Before Sam Sleeze was mayor, Corrupt Town was a quiet, peaceful little town. But everything changed. While Sam was becoming richer, the town was becoming poorer. Citizens were ____________ (18). Their air and water were ____________ (19), and their children weren't healthy. One person, Jack Powers, said, "Enough!" Powers was ____________ (20) to stop the damage.

exercise 5

Choose the correct past participles to complete this story. In some cases, there is more than one possibility. Try to use as many different participles as possible.

arrested	disgusted	scared
built	exhausted	shocked
closed	frightened	shut
concerned	interested	upset
determined	reelected	worried ✓

LOCAL HERO SAVES OUR TOWN!

Ten years ago, the Sludge Company wanted to build a factory along Crystal River. At that time, everyone in town was ___worried___ (1) about water pollution in the river, and many people protested against the factory. But our mayor, Sam

Sleeze, didn't listen. He wasn't ____________ (2) about pollution. He was really ____________ (3) in money because the Sludge Company wanted to give him a large contribution for his reelection campaign. People in town were ____________ (4) about this money, but the mayor took the money anyway.

When Mayor Sleeze was ____________ (5) and began his second term, he signed a contract with the Sludge Company. Soon, the factory was ____________ (6), and production began. Everyone in town got even more ____________ (7) about pollution when yellow and purple smoke began coming from the smokestacks, and orange and green chemicals began flowing into the river. Everyone was ____________ (8) by the horrible smells from the factory.

One young lawyer in town, Jack Powers, was very ____________ (9) about the whole situation. He was ____________ (10) to stop the pollution. He worked on this case to find laws against the mayor and against the factory. He stayed up late each night until he was ____________ (11), but finally, he found a way to close the factory and to arrest Mayor Sleeze for illegal campaign contributions. Yesterday, the Sludge Company factory was ____________ (12). And last night, Mayor Sleeze was ____________ (13) by the police while he was trying to get on a plane to Mexico.

exercise 6

What happened to the Sludge Company? What happened to Mayor Sleeze? What happened to Jack Powers? Continue the story from Exercises 4 and 5. Write a short composition. Then work in small groups. Compare your "sequels."

Using What You've Learned

activity 1

Organizing a Campaign. In small groups, choose one issue everyone in the group is concerned about. It might be about the environment, about social issues, or about politics and corruption, for example. Plan a campaign for improving the situation. Make signs or posters about the issue. Plan two or three short speeches. Finally, launch your campaign. Use the following questions to help you.

1. What problem(s) are you concerned about?
2. How can people get involved to help?
3. What specific things can you do now?
4. What should you plan for the future?
5. What might or will happen if you don't do anything now?

activity 2

Writing Letters. Choose an environmental issue you, personally, are very concerned about. Write a letter about it to a local, regional, national, or international leader. First explain the problem and then give suggestions for solutions. Finally, mail your letter!

TOPIC two
Introduction to the Present Perfect Tense

Setting the Context

prereading questions Look at the pictures. What are the people doing in each one?

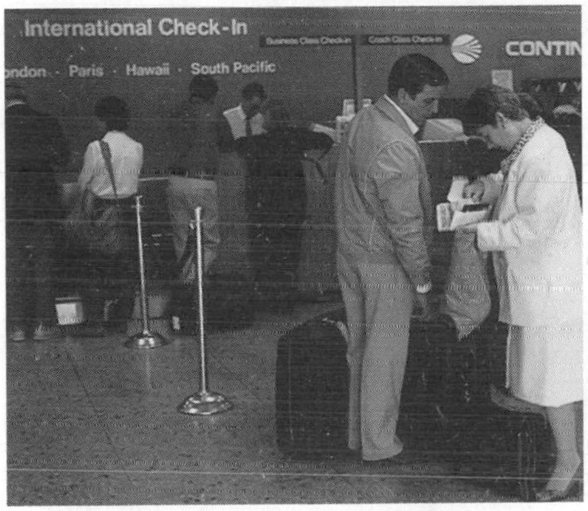

A Smaller Planet

Our planet has become smaller. Not in size, of course. It hasn't really grown smaller. But our lives have changed because we have discovered new technologies. Technological advances in travel and communications have connected the entire world. Today, we can use the telephone to call almost anyone, and we can travel by plane, boat, train, or car to almost anywhere. In the past, far away people and places were impossible to reach quickly, but no longer. Today, even the farthest places are minutes away by telephone and perhaps hours away by plane.

discussion questions

1. Is our world really smaller?
2. Why does it seem smaller? Give some examples from the passage. Then try to add some examples of your own.

A. Past Participles of Regular and Irregular Verbs

Two common uses of the past participle are in perfect tenses and in passive voice verbs. This section introduces the present perfect tense, and Topic Three introduces some passive forms.

For regular verbs, the past participle is the same as the simple past tense (verb + *ed*):

Simple forms	Simple past and past participles	Simple forms	Simple past and past participles
call	called	study	studied
happen	happened	travel	traveled
play	played	visit	visited

For irregular verbs, the past participle often changes spelling and/or pronunciation. Here is a short list of irregular past participles. See pages 308 and 309 for more irregular forms.

Simple forms	Past participles	Simple forms	Past participles
be	been	mean	meant
become	become	pay	paid
begin	begun	put	put
bring	brought	read	read
buy	bought	ride	rode
choose	chosen	run	run
come	come	say	said
do	done	see	seen
feed	fed	send	sent
fight	fought	shoot	sot
find	found	sit	sat
get	gotten	speak	spoken
give	given	spend	spent
had	had	take	taken
hold	held	teach	taught
leave	left	think	thought
make	made	win	won

exercise 1 Do not look at the verb charts on page 282. Complete the missing forms below.

SIMPLE FORMS	PAST PARTICIPLES	SIMPLE FORMS	PAST PARTICIPLES
be	been	pay	______
become	______	put	______
begin	______	______	read
bring	______	start	______
______	chosen	see	______
do	______	______	studied
find	______	______	spoken
______	gotten	take	______
______	learned	______	thought
leave	______	travel	______
make	______	visit	______

B. Present Perfect Tense: Affirmative and Negative Statements

The present perfect tense has several uses. A common use is to talk about actions in the past when we don't say or know the specific time. With the present perfect, no specific past time expression is used. Compare: *She has lived in Boston.* (present perfect) *She lived in Boston last year.* (simple past with a specific time)

Subject + *have* or *has* + past participle	**Subject + *haven't* or *hasn't* + past participle**
affirmative	**negative**
I / You / We / They } **have worked** well.	I / You / We / They } **haven't worked** there.
He / She / It } **has worked** well.	He / She / It } **hasn't worked** there.

exercise 2 Look at "A Smaller Planet" on page 281. Underline all uses of the present perfect tense. Which verbs have regular past participles? Which have irregular past participles. Write them here.

Regular Past Participles	Irregular Past Participles
have changed,	has become,

exercise 3 Make *true* statements from the following cues. Use the example as a model.

examples: **I have lived in Boston.**
I haven't lived in Madrid.

1. live
   a. in Los Angeles
   b. in Berlin
   c. in Hong Kong
   d. in Mexico City
   e. in Jakarta

2. study
   a. Spanish
   b. Math
   c. American History
   d. Chemistry
   e. Chinese

3. travel
   a. in Europe
   b. in Africa
   c. in Asia
   d. in Australia
   e. in South America

4. visit
   a. Mexico
   b. Egypt
   c. France
   d. Thailand
   e. Canada

5. try
   a. American hamburgers
   b. skiing
   c. roller blading
   d. Japanese food
   e. yoga

exercise 4 Complete the following with the past participle. Use the verbs in parentheses.

1. Technology has ___changed___ (change) our lives.
2. Technology has ______________ (help) to make travel faster, easier, and cheaper.
3. Long-distance communication has ______________ (become) faster and simpler.
4. Fax machines have ______________ (open) new possibilities for communication.
5. Telephones have ______________ (give) us a way "to stay in touch" with our friends and families from almost any place on earth.
6. Computers have ______________ (bring) many improvements in our lives.
7. More than 30 million people have ______________ (use) the Internet to communicate.
8. All of this technology has _____ (make) our planet seem much smaller.

Today, almost 100 percent of U.S. grade schools and high schools have computers and use them in the classroom.

exercise 5 Have you changed during this course? What have you done? What have you accomplished? Tell about changes in your life. Complete the sentences below with true information.

> example: During this course, **I have become more fluent in English.**

1. During this course, I have spoken . . .
2. During this class, I have become . . .
3. I have met people from . . .
4. I have made friends with . . .
5. During this course, I have tried . . .
6. I have gotten . . .
7. During this class, I have learned how to . . .
8. I have learned about . . .

C. Present Perfect Tense: Questions

Have/has + subject + past participle

yes/no questions	short answers	
	Affirmative	**Negative**
I	I	I
Have you **helped?**	Yes, you **have.**	No, you **haven't.**
we	we	we
they	they	they
he	he	he
Has she **helped?**	Yes, she **has.**	No, she **hasn't.**
it	it	it

information questions	possible answers
Who has visited Russia?	Nancy has been there twice.
How has he **helped?**	He has cleaned the entire house!
Where has she **lived?**	She has lived in five countries.
Why have they **moved?**	Because of problems with their neighbors.

exercise 6 Tell more about your experiences during this course. In pairs, ask and answer these questions.

example: Who has helped you the most during this course?
My roommate has helped me very much.

1. Who has helped you the most during this course?
2. What have you learned to do well during this semester/quarter?
3. What new foods have you tried?
4. Who have you become friends with during this course?
5. What new things have you learned about other countries and cultures?
6. What have you learned about studying languages?

exercise 7 Continue talking about your experiences. In different pairs, ask and answer these questions. Then, you can choose one question to answer in a short composition.

example: What is the most unusual thing you have done during this course?
The most unusual thing I have done is scuba diving.

1. What is the most unusual thing you have done this year?
2. What is the hardest thing you have done?
3. Who is the funniest person you have met during this course?
4. What is the best movie you have seen?
5. What is the longest story or book you have read during this course?
6. What is the prettiest place you have visited this year?
7. What is the best food you have tried recently?
8. What is the most interesting thing that you have learned (besides English grammar, of course!)?

Using What You've Learned

activity GROUP ACTIVITY

Telling About Yourself. What are the best and the worst parts of your life? What things have you done or accomplished? What has happened to you? Write at least eight statements. Use some of these categories to help you. Then work in small groups and share your experiences. Remember that you do not give a specific time in the past when you use the present perfect tense.

The Best	I have traveled around the world.
The Worst	
The Funniest	
The Most Dangerous	
The Most Difficult	
The Most Embarrassing	

TOPIC three

Introduction to the Passive Voice

Setting the Context

prereading questions Look at the picture on the next page. What is this? Where is it?

Uniting Our Planet

We have serious problems on earth, but in some important ways, our planet and its people have become more united. World organizations have brought people from many parts of the earth together, and they have made efforts to help globally. The United Nations and the International Red Cross are two primary examples. These organizations are known worldwide for their global efforts to protect and improve people's lives. The Red Cross was created in 1863 to help people in natural disasters and in wars. A Swiss, Henri Dunant, worked to create the Red Cross because he was shocked at the suffering of those who were wounded in the Battle of Solferino. The purpose of the Red Cross is to help people who are suffering because of disasters or wars, but the purpose of the United Nations is to help avoid wars in the first place. The United Nations was begun after World War II to give nations an international organization for solving differences peacefully. Today, the U.N. is involved in peace-keeping missions in many corners of the globe.

discussion questions

1. How have the United Nations and the Red Cross helped to unite countries?
2. What other international organizations do you know of?

A. Passive Versus Active Voice

Many verbs in English can use either the active or the passive voice. Compare:

Active: John mailed the letter.
The active voice focuses on the person or thing that *does* the action: *John.*

Passive: The letter was mailed (by John).
The passive voice focuses on the person or thing that *receives* the action: *The letter.*

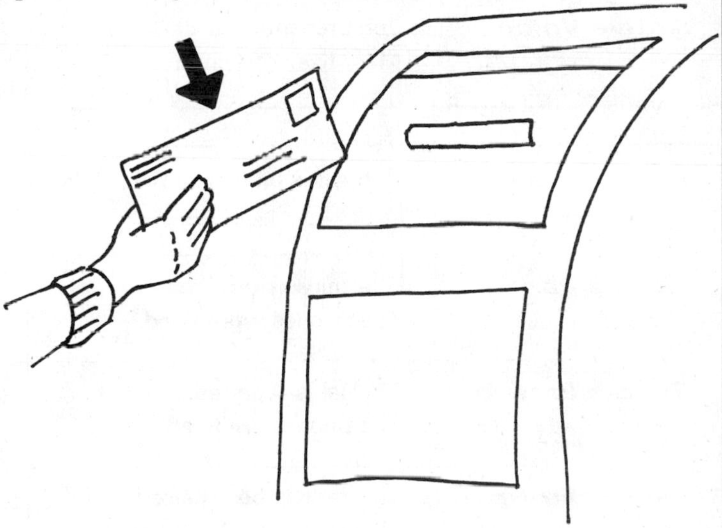

B. Phrases with *by*

In some passive sentences, it is important to know *who did* the action. These sentences use *by* + person or thing. In other passive sentences, the result of the action is more important. These sentences do not use *by*. Compare:

without *by*	with *by*
The letter was mailed.	The letter was mailed **by John, not by Sue.**
The book was written in 1973.	The book was written **by Mary Gill.**
The window was broken last week.	The window was broken **by three teenage boys in blue jeans.**

C. The Passive Voice with Simple Tenses

	affirmative	negative
Active Voice	John repaired the car. Mary fixed the phones.	John didn't repair the car. Mary didn't fix the phones.

Passive Voice	**Subject + *be* + past participle**	**Subject + *be* + *not* + past participle**
Simple Past	The car **was repaired.** The phones **were fixed.**	The car **wasn't repaired.** The phones **weren't fixed.**
Simple Present	The car **is repaired.** The phones **are fixed.**	The car **isn't repaired.** The phones **aren't fixed.**
Simple Future	The car **will be repaired.** The phones **will be fixed.**	The car **won't be repaired.** The phones **won't be fixed.**

exercise 1 Complete the following with the passive form of the verb. Use the simple past, present, or future tense.

example: pay The bill was paid yesterday.

Usually, the bills are paid at the beginning of the month.

That bill will be paid tomorrow.

1. finish project _________ yesterday.
   Their project _________ now.
   Gloria's project _________ next week.
2. elect The next president _________ a month from now.
   Jack _________ president of the club last month.
   A new president _________ every year.
3. give Jose _________ the prize last week.
   Who _________ the prize next week?
   Prizes _________ each week.
4. repair The TV _________ last week.
   The radio _________ now.
   The telephone _________ tomorrow.
5. make That decision _________ at last month's meeting.
   In general, decisions _________ at the monthly meeting.
   An important decision _________ tomorrow night.
6. do The work _________ tomorrow.
   The work _________ each week.
   The work _________ last night.

D. Common Expressions with Regular Verbs

Here are a variety of expressions that use passive voice verbs. Topic One has additional expressions.

expressions	examples
be awarded to	The prize **was awarded to** Martin.
be based on	The movie **was based on** the book.
be cancelled	The game **was cancelled** because of the rain.
be composed of	The team **is composed of** nine players.
be connected to	The video **is connected to** the TV.
be crowded (with)	The theater **was crowded with** children.
be discovered by	Radium **was discovered by** Marie Curie.
be faced with	He **was faced with** a serious problem.
be filled (with)	This paper **is filled with** mistakes.
be invented by	The steam engine **was invented by** James Watt.
be located in (at)	Stanford University **is located in** California.
be related to	Stella **is related to** the president.
be used for (as, by, with)	Scissors **are used for** cutting.
be used to + verb	A hammer **is used to** pound nails.

exercise 2

Complete these sentences with verbs in the passive voice. Use the simple past or present tense.

1. Gunpowder ___was used___ (use) by the Chinese for fireworks.
2. Gunpowder ______________ (introduce) to Europe by the Arabs.
3. The first guns ______________ (develop) by the Arabs in the 14th century.
4. Gunpowder ______________ (not use) for peaceful purposes, such as mining, until the 17th century.
5. New and powerful explosives ______________ (discover) by the Swedish chemist, Alfred Nobel, in the 1860s.
6. For example, dynamite ______________ (invent) by Nobel.
7. Nobel ______________ (concern) about the destructiveness of his invention.

8. He ______________ (interest) in using his money from dynamite to help the world.

9. The Nobel Prizes ______________ (create) to help scientists and scholars improve our world.

10. The Nobel Prize awards ______________ (start) in 1901.

11. Today, the Nobel Prize committees ______________ (locate) in Sweden and Norway.

12. The committees ______________ (compose) of Swedish and Norwegian scholars.

13. Most of the Nobel Prizes ______________ (award) in October of each year.

14. The prize money ______________ (use) for many different purposes.

E. Common Expressions with Irregular Verbs

verbs	examples
be born	Alex **was born** in July.
be chosen for (by, to)	Camila **was chosen to** represent the class.
be given to	The prize **was given to** Susan.
be known for (to)	Marina **is known for** her kind personality.
be made from (of, up of)	This shirt **is made of** cotton.
be shown	The first movie **was shown** in Paris.
be written by	*MacBeth* **was written by** Shakespeare.

exercise 3 Complete these sentences with verbs in the passive voice. Use the simple past tense. Notice that all verbs are irregular.

1. In 1964, the Nobel Peace Prize __was given__ (give) to Martin Luther King, Jr.

2. King ______________ (choose) for the award because of his work for civil rights.

3. King ______________ (bear) in the American south in 1929.
4. Most of his life ______________ (spend) working for equal rights and equal opportunities for all people.
5. In the 1950s, King ______________ (make) a Baptist minister in Montgomery, Alabama, where he worked against racial discrimination.
6. Many of his ideas ______________ (take) from Mohandas Gandhi, especially the idea of passive resistence.
7. Boycotts ______________ (begin) of segregated buses, stores, restaurants, and schools.
8. A protest march on Washington, D.C. ______________ (hold) in 1963; during this march, King made one of his most famous speeches.
9. Unfortunately, King's work ______________ (leave) unfinished.
10. He ______________ (shoot) to death in Memphis, Tennessee, on April 4, 1968.

The U.S. Civil Rights Act of 1964 officially prohibits discrimination in voting, jobs, public accommodations, and so on. However, problems with discrimination continue to exist in the United States.

exercise 1 Complete the following paragraphs with the passive voice form of the simple past, present, or future tense. Use the verbs in parentheses. Pay attention to singular and plural forms of the verb *be*.

WORLD ORGANIZATIONS

The idea of a world organization is not new. After World War I was fought (1) (fight), from 1914 to 1918, leaders from many countries were determined (2) (determine) to stop wars. The idea of a world organization was discussed (3) (discuss) soon after World War I, and the League of Nations ______ (4) (form) in 1920. It ______ (5) (locate) in Geneva, Switzerland. It ______ (6) (mean) to be a place for leaders of countries to talk to each other to stop future wars.

The League of Nations was not very successful, and it ______ (7) (disband) before World War II. After World War II, another world organization ______ (8) (propose). In 1945, the United Nations ______ (9) (begin) in San Francisco. Today, the United Nations headquarters ______ (10) (locate) in New York City.

Is the United Nations a success or failure today? It ______ (11) (say) that large countries like the United States ______ (12) (give) too much power. It is true that much of the U.N.'s budget ______ (13) (pay) by the United States. Yet, the U.N. ______ (14) (make) up of so many countries, over 190, so no country can have complete control. In any case, millions of people around the world ______ (15) (help) by this organization. World problems ______ (16) (discuss) and sometimes ______ (17) (solve), children ______ (18) (educate), families ______ (19) (feed), and sick people ______ (20) (provide) medical care, all through the efforts of the U.N.

How long will the U.N. exist in the future? No one can say. Perhaps it ______ (21) (disband) someday, like the League of Nations. But then, maybe a newer and stronger organization ______ (22) (create) in its place.

exercise 5 Complete the following story with the simple past tense. Choose the active or the passive voice. Use the verbs in parentheses.

GANDHI, A MODEL OF NONVIOLENT ACTION

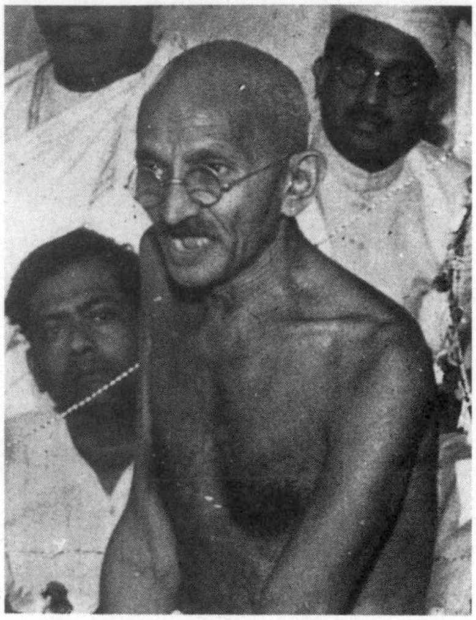

Mohandas K. Gandhi was one of the most important political activists of all time. He ___was born___ (1) (bear) in 1869, and he ___died___ (2) (die) in 1948. He ___lived___ (3) (live) in Africa and India, but he ________ (4) (know) worldwide for his work. He ________ (5) (become) famous because he ________ (6) (use) nonviolent action.

During Gandhi's life, India ________ (7) (control) by Great Britain. Even though many Indians ________ (8) (want) independence, they ________ (9) (not give) control of their country by the British. Many different ideas ________ (10) (discuss) about how to get independence. Some Indians ________ (11) (buy) guns and ________ (12) (fight) in bloody confrontations, but Gandhi ________ (13) (teach) nonviolent action.

Finally, in 1947, India ________ (14) (give) independence. Gandhi's work ________ (15) (not finish) because the new India ________ (16) (face) with many new problems. But, sadly, Gandhi ________ (17) (kill) in 1948. Gandhi's work ________ (18) (end) with his death, but his ideas and beliefs ________ (19) (remain).

Using What You've Learned

activity 1

Telling About Historical Figures. Who is a famous historical person from your country? Tell or write about the person. First, find information about his or her life. Then prepare notes or a short composition. Share the information with your classmates in small groups. Use these questions to help you prepare.

1. Who was the person?
2. When and where was the person born? Where is this place located in your country?
3. What was the person known for? Why was he or she important?
4. What examples can you give of this person's work or accomplishments?
5. How do people from your culture feel about this person today?

TOPIC four
Review

Setting the Context

prereading questions Look at the pictures and describe them. What are some of the challenges our planet is faced with in the 21st century?

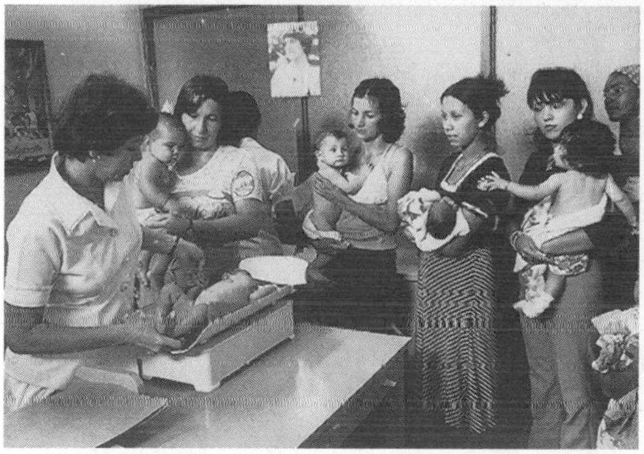

The Challenges of the 21st Century

The 20th century has brought tremendous changes to our planet. Some of these changes have made life on earth much better, but other changes have not. What will the 21st century be like? Will the 21st century bring peace and prosperity for everyone? Or will it bring suffering and destruction? What will life be like for those who come after us? What can we do today to help ensure a good future on this planet for our children and our grandchildren?

discussion questions Reread the questions at the end of the passage and give your own answers. What is your opinion?

exercise 1 Complete this conversation with the correct forms of the verbs in parentheses. Use simple present, present continuous, or future tense (active voice).

ROBERTO: Sometimes I ___hate___ (hate) to read the newspapers. The news ______1______ (be often) very depressing.

JUAN: Well, that ______2______ (not be) always true. Look at the article I ______3______ (read) right now, "Hope for Peace in the World." Some government leaders ______4______ (think) that things ______5______ (get) better now. They believe that there ______6______ (be) a better future.

ROBERTO: I ______7______ (not know). One person ______8______ (say) peace ______9______ (be) possible, but another person ______10______ (talk) about more fighting. Economic news ______11______ (not look) good either.

JUAN: I guess it all depends on your view of the world. But I ______12______ (hope) that my view is right.

exercise 2 Complete this passage with the correct forms of the verbs in parentheses. Use simple present, present continuous, simple past, or present perfect tense (active voice). In some cases, more than one tense is possible.

THE CHALLENGES WE FACE

Think about life a hundred years ago, and then think about life today. So much ___has changed___ (1) (change)! Yet, even though life ______2______ (improve) for millions of people during the 20th century, many serious problems and challenges ______3______ (face) us today. During the past one hundred years, the population of the world ______4______ (increase) dramatically, and many social, economic, and environmental problems ______5______ (develop). In 1900, the world population ______6______ (be) about 1.6 billion. By 1990, it ______7______ (be) more than 5 billion. Today, our population is ______8______ (grow) more rapidly than at any time in history. As a result, every day there ______9______ (be) more and more people, and each person ______10______ (need) food, clothing, health care, education, housing, and a healthy environment. Every person on earth ______11______ (want) a happy and healthy life. What can we and our leaders do to ensure this?

exercise 3 Think about the world today. Then complete these sentences. Use your own ideas and opinions.

1. World leaders should look for peaceful solutions.
2. Every citizen of the world should ______________________.
3. One hundred years ago, people in some parts of the world couldn't ______________________.
4. In the future, the United Nations might ______________________.
5. Government leaders don't have to ______________________.
6. Government leaders must not ______________________.
7. Of course, every person in the world would like to ______________________.
8. Every country can ______________________.
9. I would rather ______________________.

exercise 4 Put the words in the sentences in the correct order.

example: for our planet / take responsibility / all people / should

All people should take responsibility for our planet.

1. to eat better / need / many people
2. who / the hungry people / feed / can / ?
3. most of us / to bed hungry / don't go
4. some organizations / to hungry people / give food
5. to find jobs / for people / other organizations / prefer
6. all poor people / to help / we / should continue
7. will always / the world / problems / have
8. better solutions / might / find / we

exercise 5 Make questions from these sentences. The underlined words are the answers to your questions.

example: Martin Luther King, Jr., was born in <u>Atlanta, Georgia.</u>

Where was Martin Luther King, Jr., born?

1. <u>Martin Luther King, Jr.,</u> worked for equal rights for all people.
2. <u>Two hundred thousand</u> people marched in Washington, D.C., in 1963.
3. Martin Luther King, Jr., made a famous speech <u>in 1963.</u>
4. Some people hated him <u>because they were racist.</u>
5. Today more people in America have <u>better opportunities.</u>
6. No, <u>not all people have equal opportunity.</u>
7. Many people have to live <u>on the streets.</u>
8. <u>Maybe, in the future,</u> all people in the world will have equal rights.

exercise 6 Each of these sentences has one error. Find the error and correct it.

1. There ~~is~~ are a lot of problems in the world.
2. There are much good things in the world.
3. We want find solutions for world problems.
4. Some environmental problems has become very serious.
5. We are worry about pollution.
6. Water pollution is serious problem in many places.
7. Every human is needing clean water to drink.
8. Air pollution is damage historical buildings around the world.
9. Many animals and plants are endangering and might become extinct.
10. Farmers have taking land from wild animals.
11. Hunters often kill elephants for the ivory from its tusks.
12. Elephants are some of the most largest animals on earth.
13. Many environmental problems happen because need jobs and money.
14. How we can solve these problems?
15. We must to try and solve them.

Using What You've Learned

activity 1

GROUP ACTIVITY

Talking About the Future. What will be the big problems in the next fifty years? In small groups, make a list of five. What will be the big improvements? Make a list of five. Share your lists with other groups.

PROBLEMS

1. ______________________________
2. ______________________________
3. ______________________________
4. ______________________________
5. ______________________________

IMPROVEMENTS

1. ______________________________
2. ______________________________
3. ______________________________
4. ______________________________
5. ______________________________

activity 2

Talking About Your Own Future. You are finishing your English class. What will you do now? What plans do you have for the future? In small groups, take some time to tell one another about your future plans.

activity 3

Describing Your Progress in English. In pairs or small groups, talk about the progress you have made during this course. Use these questions to help you.

1. Are you pleased with your work during this course?
2. Did you get disappointed or frustrated at times? When and why?
3. Have you understood all the grammatical structures that you have studied? Are you confused about any particular structures?
4. Do you ever get bored with English grammar? (Of course not!) Are you going to take another grammar course?
5. Do you have any final comments about your class or your work?

checking your progress

Check your progress with structures from Chapters Nine and Ten. Be sure to review any problem areas.

Part 1: Choose the correct word(s) to complete each sentence.

1. Jorge _____ in Argentina.
   a. was born
   b. is born
   c. was bear
   d. born

2. The movie was _____.
   a. very boring
   b. bored
   c. very bored
   d. very bore

3. Jim is _____ photography.
   a. interesting
   b. interesting in
   c. interest
   d. interested in

4. The United Nations _____ in 1945.
   a. begun
   b. were begun
   c. beginning
   d. was begun

5. Abdul _____ chemistry.
   a. have studied
   b. has study
   c. has studied
   d. have studying

6. She _____ Madrid.
   a. has visit
   b. has visited
   c. has visiting
   d. is visited

7. John is _____ than Bjorn.
   a. as handsome
   b. handsomer
   c. more handsome
   d. handsome

8. Chris _____ the President.
   a. are related to
   b. is related to
   c. is related of
   d. are related of

9. This book is _____ that one.

- **a.** more shorter than
- **b.** shorter
- **c.** shorter than
- **d.** more short

10. Paul _____ for his skill at sports.

- **a.** is know
- **b.** is known
- **c.** known
- **d.** is knowing

Part 2: Circle the correct words to complete this story. Circle "X" to show that nothing is necessary.

Beginning a new language isn't easy, and sometimes it's very (frustrating / frustrated)[1]. Many beginning students get (boring / bored)[2], and most get very (tire / tired)[3] after listening to and speaking another language. Some people get completely (exhaust / exhausted)[4]. This is because you have to pay (X / more)[5] closer attention in a second language, or you might not understand. But later, when you become (more fluent / fluenter)[6], everything becomes (more easy / easier)[7]. Language learning is worth the effort, though. It is (say / said)[8], "One language, one man; two languages, two men." When you have (learned / learn)[9] a new language, you become a different person. You can look at life in more (as / than)[10] one way.

Appendixes

APPENDIX **one**

Parts of Speech, Sentence Parts, and Grammar Terms

Parts of Speech

The parts of speech are *adjective, adverb, article, conjunction, noun, preposition, pronoun,* and *verb.*

Noun	Verb	Article	Adjective	Noun	Preposition	Noun	Pronoun	Verb	Preposition	Noun
Mariko	is	a	young	woman	from	Japan.	She	is living	in	San Diego,

Conjunction	Pronoun	Verb	Noun	Adverb	Pronoun	Adverb	Verb	Adverb	Adverb
and	she	is studying	English	there.	She	always	studies	very	hard.

Sentence Parts

subject	verb	phrase	subject	verb	object
Mariko	is	from Japan.	Mariko	studies	English.
Mariko	studies	every night.	She	always does	her homework.

Grammar Terms

Singular	= one	a boy one dog
Plural	= two or more	boys three dogs
Subject	= the main person, place, thing, or idea in a sentence	**Mariko** came yesterday. **She** is from Japan. **Her mother** is going to visit her soon.
Verb	= an action or situation	Mariko **came** yesterday. She **is** from Japan.
Object	= the receiver of an action	Mariko met **her mother** at the airport. Mariko bought **a present** for her mother.
Phrase	= two or more words together	yesterday afternoon from Japan in the United States
Sentence	= a subject/verb combination that expresses a complete idea	Mariko came yesterday afternoon. She is from Japan. She is living in the United States. (*not:* She from Japan. She in the United States.)

APPENDIX two

Numbers and Calendar Information

Numbers

This chart gives you both the cardinal and the ordinal numbers. Note that the thirties, forties, and so on, follow the same pattern as the twenties.

cardinal	ordinal	cardinal	ordinal
zero		twenty	twentieth
one	first	twenty-one	twenty-first
two	second	twenty-two	twenty-second
three	third	twenty-three	twenty-third
four	fourth	twenty-four	twenty-fourth
five	fifth	twenty-five	twenty-fifth
six	sixth	twenty-six	twenty-sixth
seven	seventh	twenty-seven	twenty-seventh
eight	eighth	twenty-eight	twenty-eighth
nine	ninth	twenty-nine	twenty-ninth
ten	tenth	thirty	thirtieth
eleven	eleventh	forty	fortieth
twelve	twelfth	fifty	fiftieth
thirteen	thirteenth	sixty	sixtieth
fourteen	fourteenth	seventy	seventieth
fifteen	fifteenth	eighty	eightieth
sixteen	sixteenth	ninety	ninetieth
seventeen	seventeenth	(one) hundred	(one) hundredth
eighteen	eighteenth	(one) thousand	(one) thousandth
nineteen	nineteenth	(one) million	(one) millionth

Calendar Information

days of the week		months of the year		seasons
Sunday	Sun.	January	Jan.	Winter
Monday	Mon.	February	Feb.	Spring
Tuesday	Tues.	March	Mar.	Summer
Wednesday	Wed.	April	Apr.	Autumn or Fall
Thursday	Thurs.	May		
Friday	Fri.	June		
Saturday	Sat.	July		
		August	Aug.	
		September	Sept.	
		October	Oct.	
		November	Nov.	
		December	Dec.	

APPENDIX three

Irregular Verbs

simple form	past	past participle	simple form	past	past participle
be	was / were	been	leave	left	left
bear	bore	born	lend	lent	lent
become	became	become	lose	lost	lost
begin	begun	begun	make	made	made
bite	bit	bitten	mean	meant	meant
blow	blew	blown	meet	met	met
break	broke	broken	pay	paid	paid
bring	brought	brought	put	put	put
build	built	built	read	read	read
buy	bought	bought	ride	rode	ridden
catch	caught	caught	ring	rang	rung
choose	chose	chosen	run	run	run
come	came	come	say	said	said
cost	cost	cost	see	saw	seen
do	did	done	sell	sold	sold
draw	drew	drawn	send	sent	sent
drink	drank	drunk	shake	shook	shaken
drive	drove	driven	shoot	shot	shot
eat	ate	eaten	shut	shut	shut
fall	fell	fallen	sing	sang	sung
feed	fed	fed	sit	sat	sat
feel	felt	felt	sleep	slept	slept
fight	fought	fought	speak	spoke	spoken
find	found	found	spend	spent	spent
fly	flew	flown	stand	stood	stood
forget	forgot	forgotten	steal	stole	stolen
freeze	froze	frozen	sweep	swept	swept
get	got	gotten	swim	swam	swum
give	gave	given	take	took	taken

simple form	past	past participle	simple form	past	past participle
go	went	gone	teach	taught	taught
grow	grew	grown	tear	tore	torn
hang	hung	hung	tell	told	told
have	had	had	think	thought	thought
hear	heard	heard	throw	threw	thrown
hit	hit	hit	understand	understood	understood
hold	held	held	win	won	won
hurt	hurt	hurt	write	wrote	written
keep	kept	kept			
know	knew	known			

Index